MW01275760

Agoraphobia

You have the power in your hands to take your life back

End Anxiety and Stop Panic Attacks Fast

Demetra Harlington

CONTENTS

Table of Contents

i

CHAPTER ONE

Imagine living in a constant state of panic. A state where everything ranging from shopping malls to public spaces puts you in a position of extreme fear and worry that you become so scared of living your home. This was the case of Martin, a 23 year old from Denver.

As Martin would tell it, he wasn't always so scared. Yes, he got worried sometimes and he was a bit claustrophobic but that was the extent of it. He was a pretty normal guy up until the age of 19. On the first day of college, in the midst of a lot of people, he had his first full blown panic attack. Rooted to the ground unable to breathe with the sensation of a million needles pricking his arm, he passed out.

Rushed to the hospital, nothing seemed to be wrong with him and his experience was chalked up to be as a result of nerves. This explanation was fine until he had the same experience in a grocery store two weeks later.

Going on a few years, his panic attacks gave him no room for a normal life. He couldn't step out of his room, public spaces terrified him and people avoided him because his condition just didn't seem normal.

Luckily for him, his friend was a psychology major. A lot of weeks spent planning and millions of panic attacks later, he was able to make it to the therapist office where he underwent tests and endured numerous questions from the doctor, he was diagnosed with a condition called AGORAPHOBIA.

WHAT IS AGORAPHOBIA

Agoraphobia is also called the "fear of fear". It is

described as intense fear of places and situations in which running away or escape might be difficult or extremely humiliating if he/she develops symptoms of panic. Such places could include shopping malls, restaurants, public malls, public cars, crowds or open places. It could also include waiting in line, traveling far from home or even being alone. Although panic attacks are usually feared, some other symptoms which arises fear in the individuals include loss of bladder and/or bowel control, vomiting and headaches.

The Diagnostic and Statistical Manual of Mental Disorders (fourth edition) also known as the *DSM-IV-TR*, which is the standard handbook used by mental health professionals to diagnose mental health describe patients with agoraphobia as being afraid of symptoms such as dizziness, sudden attack of diarrhea and fainting spells or being labelled as crazy by the society.

HISTORY OF AGORAPHOBIA

The term 'Agoraphobia' was coined from two greek words- 'Agora' which means marketplace and 'Phobia' which means fear. The marketplace also represents a place of assembly or open space.

This term is linked to a German Psychologist called Carl Friedrich Otto Westphal who introduced the term when he published an article titled "Agoraphobia: the neuropathic phenomenon" at the end of the nineteenth century in the year 1871. In his article, he described people who were scared of crossing open spaces and going to public places like squares, theatres or churches as agoraphobic. However, the condition was not widely recognized until the late 1970s.

The term Agoraphobia appeared for the first time in the Diagnostic and Statistical Manual of Mental disorders in the third edition (DSM-III). Agoraphobia as of then was considered to be a primary diagnosis which may or may not be accompanied by continuous panic attacks.

Over the years, there has been an attempt by authors,doctors and mental health professionals to categorize this disorder. The relationship between agoraphobia and panic disorder was heavily contended. Some scientists viewed it as a category of panic disorder and denied the possibility of its existence without panic. Others viewed the disorder as a separate disorder from panic attacks.

BASIC FACTS ABOUT AGORAPHOBIA

A study conducted showed that agoraphobia without panic disorder is more common than agoraphobia with panic disorder. The lifetime prevalence for agoraphobia with panic disorder was estimated at 5.3%. Also, a survey carried out by the Epidemiological catchment area (ECA) which was based on DSM-III specifications reported a 4.3% lifetime prevalence of agoraphobia without panic disorder.

In a survey done in 1993 by Horwarth and his fellow researchers, about 22 people suffering from agoraphobia with panic disorder were randomly interviewed. Out of those 22 people, only two received an actual diagnosis of agoraphobia without panic disorder, one of which have subclinical panic attacks. The remaining participants were reclassified into special phobias, panic disorders, etc.

Agoraphobia is often quite disabling. An NCS study was conducted, and only 26.5% of people reported that the disorder had a huge negative impact on their lives, and severe impairment of the body's function is most common among victims of the disorder.

DEMOGRAPHIC

Survey done in 2017 by the 'National Comorbidity Survey Replication' showed that approximately 0.9% of US citizens (approximately 1.8 million people) had agoraphobia in the year 2017 with a slight difference between males and females (0.9% for females, 0.8% for males). This was different from the previous years when the rate of incidence was higher in females. The reason for the higher number of females than males when it comes to avoidance could be cultural and gender differences. The tendency of an agoraphobic to avoid situations and environment seems to be inversely proportional to the masculinity scores. This means that a higher masculinity score resulted in a lower rate of avoidance.

The survey results also showed that approximately 1.3% of US adults experience agoraphobia at one point or the other of their lives. The average age of commencement of the disease is approximately 29 years and the incidence rate in teenagers is approximately 2.4 million.

Panic disorders often begins at mid-teens and is often absent at childhood.

REFERENCES

1. Bienvenu O.J., Wuyek, L.A., Stein, M.B. (2010). Anxiety disorders diagnosis: some history and controversies. Current Topics in Behavioral Neurosciences **2** (3-19)

2. Aqeel, Noorulain, et al. "A Strange Case of Agoraphobia: A Case Study." Insight Medical Publishing Group, Insight Medical Publishing Group, 19 Oct. 2016.

3. American Psychiatric Association. Diagnostic and Statistical Manual of Mental Disorders. 4th edition, text revised.Washington, DC: American Psychiatric Association,2000.

Agoraphobia

CHAPTER TWO

WHAT TO KNOW ABOUT PANIC ATTACKS

Panic attacks are defined as unexpected attacks not caused by ingestion of substances, medication or medical conditions. A panic attack has the sufferer experiencing symptoms such as quickened and irregular heartbeats, dizziness, inability to breathe and paralyzing fear. This feeling was a regular experience for Katie, a 45 year old from New Jersey.

At the age of 32, she experienced her first ever panic attack sitting on the bed reading as was her custom. As she described it, it started with her heart suddenly beating erratically. Her eyes became blurry and she just couldn't see the words anymore. Next thing she felt was the sudden rise in her body temperature-she felt so hot and all she could think of was trying to get her body back under control.

As she ran to the bathroom to pour water all over her body, the shaking increased. Along with it came a sudden terrifying thought-"This is the end". This thought scared her even more than what was happening to her. The thought of never seeing her family, dying without anyone around her, these thoughts were more paralyzing. Her heart began to beat faster than anything she had ever seen, her breaths became sharper, her eyes became darker. Sinking to the ground, she lost all sense of timing as she waited for her imminent death.

Katie's experience is similar to the experience of about 3.1 percent of the US adult population and approximately 13.2% of the world population.

WHAT HAPPENS IN THE BRAIN DURING A PANIC ATTACK

According to research, a panic attack is often as a result of your fight or flight response being set off intensely for a short time period. A panic attack is triggered by a feeling of fear whether real or imagined. People suffering from panic attacks often feel like they are either on the verge of death, about to choke or just going crazy. Others also report feeling like they are on the verge of a heart attack. These episodes often reach their peak in about 10 minutes and end within half an hour.

For many years, scientists have been trying to discover what happens in the brain of a person suffering from panic attacks. In 1989, Gorman and other scientists like himself published an article titled "A neuroanatomical hypothesis for panic disorder". He proposed that there was a neuroanatomic pathway which explained Panic anxiety.

Some of the structures mentioned in their research included the amygdala, hippocampus and hypothalamus, thalamus, brainstem structures (e.g., the locus coeruleus (LC), PAG, parabrachial nucleus), and cortical structures.

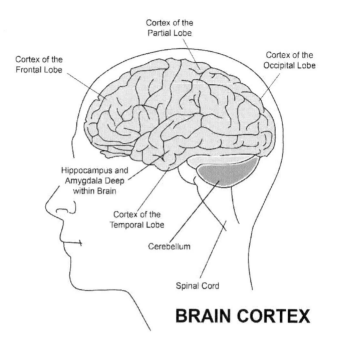

BRAIN CORTEX

SOME STRUCTURES OF THE BRAIN INVOLVED IN PANIC ATTACKS

According to his theory, the brainstem structures (locus coeruleus, parabrachial nucleus and PAG) controlled the actual panic felt by the individual.while anticipatory anxiety was mediated by the limbic systems.

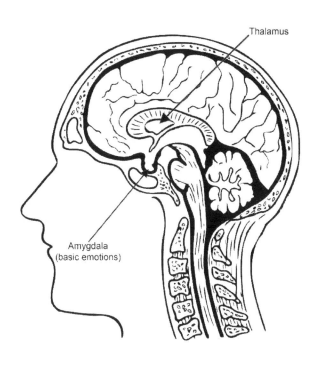

THE LOCUS COERULEUS AND ITS ROLE IN AROUSAL

One of the first responses observed in a state of fear and anxiety is autonomic activation and increased level of arousal. A theory proposed was that the noradrenergic system which arises from the locus coeruleus is the basis of which all feelings of fear and anxiety arise.

The locus coeruleus contains a huge amount of

noradrenaline cell bodies found in the brain. Its role, which is to respond to alarming and stressful stimuli is highly important. In animals such as cats or monkeys, increased firing of neurons in the locus coeruleus is associated with alertness, vigilance and selective attention to meaningful stimuli.

Recent information suggests that in a relaxed state, the locus coeruleus just promotes selective attention while firing of neurons from the locus coeruleus in a tensed state produces high behavioral attentiveness.

Some neurons from the locus coeruleus are projected to the paraventricular nucleus in the hypothalamus to activate the hypothalamic pituitary-adrenocortical axis triggering the stress response which is associated with increasing levels of anxiety.

Noradrenergic neurons also project to the central part of the amygdala, the prefrontal cortex, the base of the stria terminalis, the hippocampus, the periaqueductal gray, the hypothalamus, thalamus and the nucleus tractus solitarius. All these areas are involved in fear and anxiety. In return, the locus coeruleus is innervated by areas such as the amygdala, which is involved in processing fear based stimuli

It is one of the major sources of norepinephrine which mobilizes the body for action in cases like fight or flight reactions.

THE SEPTOHIPPOCAMPAL SYSTEM

One of the first manifestations of a fearful and anxious state is the inhibition of ongoing behaviours. In the 1970s, a scientist named Gray suggested that vulnerability to anxiety is associated with individual differences in the activity of a septohippocampal behavioural inhibition system (BIS). The main function of the BIS is to compare actual and expected stimuli and take notes of discrepancies.

If there is any uncertainty between the actual and unexpected stimuli, the BIS is activated leading to arousal and attention to new environmental stimuli is increased.

Another scientist called Laborit associated anxiety with the stress response. He believed that anxiety appears when one realises that it is impossible to take proper adaptive action and has thus lost control over the issue and it depends on the activation of the HPA axis.

Another researcher called Panksepp argues that the activities of the noradrenaline systems and the BIS are correlated and supportive systems that participate in the numerous rain readjustments or changes regarding fear and anxiety,

These systems participate in the start of fear and anxiety behaviours with the noradrenaline system involved in the alarm reaction which occurs at the beginning whereas the septohippocampal inhibition causes freezing which helps regulate the intensity and time of fear.

AMYGDALA:

In any mammal, there are three sites where electric simulations in the brain will provide a full fear response. These sites are:

- The lateral and central zone of the amygdala
- Anterior and medial hypothalamus
- Specific areas of the PAG

A circuit coursing from the lateral and central nuclei of the amygdala, the anterior and medial hypothalamic areas down to the mesencephalic PAG makes up the main fear system since freezing as well as flight and other symptoms of fear namely increased heart rate, and eliminative behavior can be evoked along the whole trajectory of this system.

The amygdala containing 13 nuclei is segregated into the lateral, basal and central subregions. In humans, the amygdala nuclei are grouped into three different subgroups-cortical, latero-basal (lateral and basal nuclei) and centromedial subgroup.

These subgroups control the fear pathway. Any disturbance in the amygdalmic ares and any of its connections lead to magnified fear and anxiety responses such as panic attacks, illogical worrying, and anxiousness.

The amygdala plays a major role by grouping rapid, direct, thalamic input into one whole. In other words, it gives more information

In patients exhibiting extreme panic attacks, MRI

scans showed a great reduction in the size of the amygdala, especially the right side. This is because the right hemisphere is theorized to be in greater control of emotions, in this case, fear than the left.

Studies also show that the right amygdala has a role in processing acquired fear while the left amygdalae major role is in processing innate fear. There was also an increased activity in the right amygdala of patients with panic attacks .

Surprisingly, there is also a sex difference in the amygdala according to the strength of the expressions. Happy faces produced greater activity in the right than left amygdala in males but this was not the case not for females.

The amygdala plays a major role in conditioning process in behavioral development (controlling emotional behavior). If a person has been exposed to a stimulus inducing fear, the person will experience a state of conditioned fear when the stimulus is present. Activation of the amygdala by affecting the stimuli influences cognitive processes alongside selective attention, perception and explicit memory.

HIPPOCAMPUS

The hippocampus is derived from the word 'Seahorse' in Greek. An easy description of this part of the brain is a 'seahorse shaped structure found in the deep parts of the brain'. It was first called "Cornu ammoinis" named after Ammon, an egyptian god near the temple of lake ammon.

The hippocampus plays a huge role in memory development, acquisition and coordinating information of complex environment (spatial cognition). It is also one of the first organs to be damaged in alzheimer's disease.

However, recent discovery brought up something new about the hippocampus. Some study done recently showed that the anterior hippocampus, which is located at the anterior (front) region of the hippocampus has a hand in emotional regulation.

Another study also showed that during a panic attack, the anxiety cells found in the ventral hippocampus become hyperexcitable. The more excitable the anxiety cells are, the more agitated and fearful the person or animal becomes. The hippocampus also controls the hypothalamic pituitary adrenal axis which is in turn activated by the amygdala causing a panic attack.

PREFRONTAL CORTEX

The main role of the prefrontal cortex is to analyse complex stimuli or situations and control emotional responses.

The prefrontal cortex controls septohippocampal security and lesions to this area could damage processing of vital information for the subicular comparator (Hippocampus) subsequently affecting behavioural inhibition and anticipatory anxiety.

The various subdivisions of the human prefrontal cortex (dorsomedial, ventrolateral and orbital roles) have specific roles in controlling emotional responses.

However, there are important differences between

right and left side of the prefrontal cortex within each of these sectors. More studies using a PET (Positron emission spectrography) have shown that negative effect and anxiety are associated with increased activation of the right prefrontal cortex.

SUMMARY

The basis for fear and anxiety are now recognized and the major brain structures and neuronal circuits involved in emotional processing and behavior are explained in full.

Stressors cause the locus coeruleus to release norepinephrine to these panic causing organs while also triggering the sympathetic neurons (leading to increased heart beat, dilated pupils, and increased perspiration) and the HPA axis through other neurotransmitters.

The released norepinephrine acts on the heart (increasing heart rate) and the lungs (tightening the bronchioles) heightening the symptoms of the attack.

The amygdala triggers the hypothalamus in the throes of a panic attack causing the release of Corticotropin releasing factor which activates the adrenocorticotropic hormone which leads to the secretion of cortisol from the adrenal cortex in the kidney.

Cortisol increases the level of glucose in the blood giving more energy to the neurons and nuclei aiding the panic attack

Another symptom of a panic attack is hyperventilation and a powerlessness to even catch and hold your breath. This is because the amygdala which has been triggered by fear activates the parabrachial nucleus. As you try to breathe more, you automatically start to breathe through your chest or diaphragm leading to inhalation of excessive carbon dioxide leading to a state of alkalosis

Dizziness, lethargy, fainting spells, headaches, pin

and needle feeling along your arm-all of these are a side effect of Alkalosis

MODELS OF AGORAPHOBIA

BIOLOGICAL MODEL

The main reason for the development of this model has come from Klein's model of anxiety and agoraphobia which focuses on the role of spontaneous panic attacks.

In 1960, Klein and his co workers noted the effect of antidepressants on patients who suffer from recurrent anxiety. After this observation, Klein then postulated a new theory of pathological anxiety based on a distinction between panic and chronic anxiety.

Klein segregated anxiety into chronic and panic anxiety. He defined panic attacks as spontaneous and out of the blue attacks which often represent a biological dysfunction. Chronic anxiety, also known as anticipatory anxiety is triggered by certain stimuli or the anticipation of it and more often than not, occurs in feared situations or in anticipation of them.

Klein provided a new insight into agoraphobia using this model. He used this model to describe agoraphobia as the fear of fear i.e. panic attacks. It is the model used as prototype in the understanding of agoraphobia.

Klein gives five major arguments for the validity of his model. They are:

- Drug specificity: Different drugs are used for both panic and chronic anxiety. Tricyclic antidepressants are used to treat panic anxiety but not chronic anxiety. Sedatives and other minor tranquilizers do not affect panic attacks but treat chronic anxiety.
- Panic induction: Panic can be induced by a sodium lactate fusion in panicked people
- Family studies: Family and twin data shows a greater genetic factor for panic attacks as opposed to anticipatory anxiety.
- Spontaneity of panic attacks: Most panic attacks start at the beginning as very spontaneous attacks not as a reaction to specific stimuli
- Separation anxiety: About half of all agoraphobic patients have a history of separation anxiety.

COGNITIVE MODEL OF AGORAPHOBIA

This model is based on an assessment of the main cause of assessment as a threat assessment. This means that an individual assesses the threat and overestimates it making it bigger than it actually is and then interpret the physical sensations gotten to mean they are about to face imminent danger. They also feel incapable of dealing with the threat if it comes up. This thought process is as a result of negative beliefs existing earlier.

According to Clark, 1998, this is due to the body's ability to interpret a situation as way more dangerous than they originally are. An example could be misinterpreting a jittery shaky feeling for losing control and going crazy.

Some of the major problems which leads to fear includes fainting, panic attack, dizziness, Once this threat is thought to be bigger than it actually is, the person provides one or all of the counter reactions

- Extreme attention to the threat causing stimuli
- Awakening physiological defense mechanisms
- Safety seeking behaviours

Some of the behaviours exhibited isnt necessarily just avoiding the environment, but also going through all kinds of torture in a bid to reduce or prevent unpleasant feelings altogether.

The reactions exhibited do nothing to reduce the impact of the threat belief but rather increases or maintains the significance of the threat belief. As the condition progresses with the panic and avoidance increasing, it becomes difficult to remember the original reason for the panic.

The major criticism of this model is that it is unclear about theories and concepts that might not be testable.

RELATIONSHIP BETWEEN PANIC DISORDER AND AGORAPHOBIA

Panic disorder is a condition characterized by a person repeatedly getting panic attacks. Panic attacks are divided into three types mainly:

- Unexpected panic attacks: These kinds of attacks comes unexpectedly and without warning. In most cases, nothing triggers the attack
- Situationally bound attack: These kinds of attacks are often linked to a particular situation. Even thinking about the situation can bring up an attack.
- Situational predisposed attack: Often similar to situational bound attacks but in this case, the panic attack might or might not be triggered by situations.

Previously, in the DSM-1V classification of mental disorders, there were three separate diagnoses of agoraphobia

- Panic disorder with agoraphobia
- Agoraphobia without panic disorder
- Agoraphobia without history of panic disorder.

PANIC DISORDERS WITHOUT AGORAPHOBIA:

The DSM-IV defines panic disorder without agoraphobia as a disorder in which patients are repeatedly plagued by panic attacks. This causes the affected individual to worry about having the attack for a month or so and might therefore, change his patterns and habits.

In other words, a patient who feels the pins and needles sensation might go into a frenzy trying to prevent a heart attack.As always, patients with panic attack like to be in control. Most patients who have gone through a panic disorder, are always afraid of looking crazy

According to the DSM-IV, before an attack is considered a panic attack, one or more of the symptoms below must have repeatedly occurred.

- Sweaty hands with rapid heart beat
- Excessive and uncontrolled
- Chills or unusual hot flushes
- Shaking of the body and lethargy
- Coughing and Choking

- Chest pain or discomfort along the thoracic (chest) region
- Nausea or abdominal pain
- Dizziness, unsteadiness, lightheadedness or faintness
- Derealization (A feeling of being in a different plane or time) or depersonalization (Detachment from oneself. Some people describe it as watching away from your body)
- Illogical and extreme fear of having a panic attack and losing control thus seeming crazy
- Fear of death
- Paresthesias (numbness or tingling sensation-pins and needles)
- Chills or hot flashes

Other criteria for a panic attack to be considered as separate from agoraphobia is :

1. The panic attacks must not be as a physiological result of any   medication, drug abuse or medical condition.
2. The panic attacks not better explained using other disorders Like social disorders, social or specific phobias or obsessive compulsive disorder.

AGORAPHOBIA WITH PANIC DISORDER

This is the type of agoraphobia which is widely known. People who experience these types of disorders often encounter their disorder in one of two different ways

- They might experience sudden fits of anxiety. This causes a feeling of dread to go to a public place where medical help might not be readily available
- They become so scared of further attacks that they become housebound. A person whose attack is usually triggered in grocery stores or markets tends to avoid stores and markets.

The DSM-IV also adds other criteria before any panic attack can be recognized as a panic attack with agoraphobia. However, these criteria are similar to the ones listed in the panic attack without agoraphobia.

However, a new update in the year 2013 to the classification of mental health disorders (DSM-5) changed the classification of anxiety and panic disorders leaving some questions in its wake.

The DSM-5 reclassified panic attacks. Previously, panic attacks were categorized into situationally bound, situationally predisposed and unexpected. However, the new classification of panic attack Is separated into:

- Expected panic attacks: These panic attacks are triggered by a specific fear. An example of one of such fears is the fear of speaking in public
- Unexpected panic attacks: Are apparently not triggered or cued by any logical reason and more often than not, seems to appear out of the blue.

Another main update in the recent DSM-5 classification is the separation of panic attacks from agoraphobia. In other words, the two are being treated as separate disorders with no relationship at all between them.

For a person to be diagnosed as having agoraphobia, the person must have experienced an intense anxiety in two situations involving stepping out into public spaces, or crowds

REFERENCE

1. American Psychiatric Association. Diagnostic and Statistical Manual of Mental Disorders. *5th ed.* Washington D.C.:2013

2. Kaufman J, Charney D. Comorbidity of mood and anxiety disorders. Depress Anxiety 2000;12(suppl 1): 69-76.

3. Gorman JM, Ken JM, Sullivan GM, Coplan JD. Neuroanatomic hypothesis of panic disorder, revised. Am J Psychiatry 2000;157: 493-505.

4. Roth WT, Wilhelm FH, Pettit D. Are current theories of panic falsifiable? Psychol Bull 2005;131: 171-92.

Agoraphobia

CHAPTER THREE

A friend of mine recently told me the story of Macy, a 23-old agoraphobia patient who has been unable to leave the house for 3 years.

According to Macy, Agoraphobia is similar to a dictator in chief. You completely relinquish control of your body and emotions to it and it tells you where to go, who to see, and what to do. It demands that you give up your independence, your hopes, your dreams and live under its control for as long as you let it.

Hearing Macy talk, It was easy to realise that she wasn't always like that. She was a shy child but at least she could leave the house and actually make friends. The disorder seemed to suddenly sneak up on her when she wasn't noticing, but she believes it must have started in the 6th grade. This was how she recalled it

Excited and scared, she stepped into the twelfth

grade with the fervent hope that things were going to get better. She knew she was never going to be Miss Popular but she prayed for this class to go smoothly for her. Her prayers were not answered.

In the first period alone, she had heard over twenty names being hurled at her. She had never felt so alone especially when she turned and saw the remaining students laughing at her. She was walking home that day when she had her first ever panic attack.

When asked to describe how she felt, she described it as an outer-body experience. As she walked, she found herself continuously zoning out and feeling faint. At the beginning, she thought she was coming down with something until the panic began. She suddenly began to feel the walls close in around her. She ran the remaining distance home and all the while she was running, she kept thinking about dying on the road without anyone being able to find her.

She didn't experience this feeling again and concluded it was just a figment of her imagination until it happened as she walked home from school again and on this day, there was no seeming trigger and it came as a surprise to her.

She said it started as a feeling of detachment followed by the feeling of zoning out. She felt unsafe, uneasy and consumed with fright for no apparent reason. Her body felt hot and shaky and she suddenly found herself drenched in sweat.This experience left her more rattled than the other one had and she found herself starting to get scared to go to school.

The next time she felt an attack was in a bus visiting a friend the next town over. She felt panicked, her palms felt clammy and all she could do was count her breath repeatedly to stop herself from keeling over. Her stomach felt as if it was tied in knots and her mind kept replaying images of how she was going to die without one of her family members in sight.

She describes the sense of relief she felt getting down from the bus as greater than anything she had ever felt. She didn't even hear other people calling her as she ran to the house of the person they were there to visit.

After the visit, as she planned to go home, she was filled with a mind crippling terror. She was so scared of getting into another bus to go home but she had no choice.

Once she came home, everybody noticed the difference in her. Never extremely outgoing, this time, she had withdrawn into her own shell refusing to come out. The little social life she had died, she couldn't go anywhere else except school and even that had her filled with nerves.

The only constant safe space she had was her room and she spent hours in there. She was scared of the panic attack that was sure to happen whenever she took a public transport, or entered a place without a very noticeable exit and entry point. She was even scared of meeting new people and fell into a panic attack whenever she was close to or introduced to someone even remotely new to her.

CAUSES OF AGORAPHOBIA

Agoraphobia as discussed earlier is caused by a fear of repetitive panic attacks. The person unconsciously links the environment or trigger to the panic attack and becomes extra scared of exposing themselves to that trigger again.

The fear they feel morphs into another panic attack whenever they are in similar situations or environment. This increases the fear of the person for that situation or environment resulting in a loop.

A lot of studies have been done on the topic agoraphobia to determine the exact causes of the disorder and some findings. Currently, the exact cause of agoraphobia is not known, however, research pinpoints several factors which can contribute to the condition.

Some of the factors could include genetic factors, inner temperament, physiological reaction to stress, life events, learned behavior and gender role socialization.

GENETIC FACTORS

Agoraphobia is more prevalent in females as compared to males with a mean inception age of 25 years.

Studies on families and twins have provided constant proof on family and genetics as one of the major factors of agoraphobia and anxiety disorders as a whole.

The major way this research is performed is through a process called 'family studies'. In this experiment, the regularity of the disorder (agoraphobia and panic disorder) among relatives of affected people is compared to relatives of unaffected controls.

Currently, six similar family studies research have been performed on people with panic disorder and agoraphobia have been performed. These studies show an increased rate of panic attacks at a rate of 5-16% in relatives of affected individuals. The studies also shows that there was a higher risk (17%) of panic disorder and agoraphobia in first degree relatives of affected subjects who are about the age of 20. However, the risk drops to only six percent when the affected person is above 20 years of age. These studies also show that the risk of the disorder increases in first degree relatives by seven percent when compared to others.

With the aim of differentiating environmental and genetic contributions, another research was conducted with a focus on twins this time. This study focused on the similarity rates of the disorder in monozygotic (identical) twins and dizygotic (fraternal) twins. The first study done in 2001 estimated that panic disorder was inherited at a rate of 43% among monozygotic twins as compared to fraternal twins. The result supports gene as a factor involved in transmission of agoraphobia.

Recently, studies also show that there is a genetic component to agoraphobia which can be separated from its relationship to panic disorder. A Yale research team of geneticists in 2001 reported uncovering a genetic locus on chromosome 3. This loci controls the susceptibility of a person to developing agoraphobia. Two loci were also found to be linked to panic disorder-the first one on chromosome 1 and the other on chromosome 11q.

These set of researchers hence concluded that there is a relationship between panic disorder and agoraphobia in that they are both genetic disorders that can be inherited and share some of the genetic loci responsible for susceptibility.

INNER TEMPERAMENT

In a bid to learn more about the cause of the condition, researchers considered the role of temperament in agoraphobia and panic disorder.

Researchers strongly consider neuroticism and extravertism as one of the main factors in the formation of anxiety disorders. Some researchers strongly believe that neuroticism is closely related to negative feelings while extraversion often or not results in a more positive effects and positive behaviour.

There is a theory postulated that neuroticism directly influences negative emotions such as anxiety and sadness while the extraversion temperament is directly linked to being sociable, increased levels of anxiety and positive emotions such as excitement and joy.

The belief that there is a relationship between temperament and emotional disorders arises from the 'Tripartite model'. This model propounds that neuroticism is related to anxiety and mood disorders while the extraversion temperament is surprisingly related to depression.

In 2001, a research was performed using logistic regression to examine the effect of extraversion on lifetime occurrence of anxiety and emotional disorders. Results showed that there was an inverse relationship between extraversion and mood disorders. In other words, lower levels of extraversion (high introversion) were linked with increased lifetime agoraphobia levels.

There was no significant relationship however between extraversion and panic disorder. Also, the results obtained showed that low levels of extraversion described panic disorder with agoraphobia but not panic disorder without agoraphobia. What this could mean is that while extraversion could result in the formation of agoraphobia with panic disorder, it could not develop the panic disorder itself.

Another temperament tested is the anxiety sensitivity which is the fear of anxiety and symptoms related to anxiety. Scientists wanted to determine the relationship between anxiety sensitivity, neuroticism and extraversion. It was determined that an increased levels of anxiety sensitivity develops during puberty and coexists with an increased maintenance of panic disorder. In other words, people with higher levels of anxiety sensitivity experience a greater range of panic

PHYSIOLOGICAL REACTION TO ILLNESS

A researcher called Godwin and his fellow researchers called attention to the relationship between panic disorder (agoraphobia) and respiratory obstructive disorders in the year 2003. Critical levels of respiratory obstructive disorders were linked with an increased likeliness of any panic disorder possibly occurring.

The research proved that asthma increases the level of panic disorder through the mechanism explained below

(i) It produces threatening sensations in the body of individuals by making breathing extremely difficult and reducing the suffocation threshold in the body. This then creates panic and fearful beliefs among individuals in the person's mind leading them to exaggerate the significance of their respiratory impairment.

STRESSFUL LIFE EVENTS

Approximately 42% of people suffering from agoraphobia report having gone through a stressful life event.

A research conducted in 2011 to determine the effect of stressful life events and agoraphobia. Results showed a lasting effect caused by family/ household events on the test subjects' panic level (worsening the severity of their panic symptoms)

Some examples of stressful life events include:

- Family arguments
- Arguments with close friends
- Feeling of abandonment by people held dear
- Demotion at work
- Being fired from a place of work
- Change of jobs

These results proved that there was a relationship between threat to interpersonal relations and financial stability with increased risk of raised panic levels. Stressful life events trigger an inner biological predisposition to panic attack. A serious family argument could lead to higher risks of hyperventilation that leads to hyperventilation.

Another theory postulates that individual difference as regards to sensitivity to stressful life events determines panic attack levels. In other words, some individuals are able to handle stressful life events better than other people.

LEARNED BEHAVIOURS

In an experiment conducted by Bouton et al, the causative factors of panic disorder with special attention on classical condition was highlighted. The main aim of the research was to determine the relationship between two negative emotions namely anxiety and panic.

Panic attacks seem to be a common component in the society probably as a reaction to stress. This reaction is termed a 'false alarm'. However, the alarm being fault does not affect the workings of classical condition. These clues become externalised often in the form of external environments such as malls or open space. The clues could also become internalised causing hyperventilation and panic attacks to occur. What this means is that in the absence of an external sensation, the body embodies the internal sensations that accompanied the earlier condition as a threat.

Observation shows that panic disorder occur more in females than males. In a research conducted by Weissman *et al.*, 1985, 65% of people suffering from agoraphobia are women.It also shows that women fall into the avoidance cycle way more than males do while men use other methods to drown out the panic felt.

One of the main explanations of the gender imbalance in females is the cultural factor where women according to the traditional gender roles are allowed to become housebound while men drown their panic in a bottle of alcohol.

ATTACHMENT THEORY

The attachment is a model which tries to describe the workings of long term and short term interpersonal relationships between humans. It describes how humans behave in relationships when hurt, separated from loved ones or in threat of danger.

Bowlby in 1969 determines that human children is attached with an 'attachment behavioural system' which makes sure that there is a certain closeness to one or more caretaker for survival to occur. He proposes that the child has working models of their relationship to their caretakers. The working models signifies the child's expectation of a relationship with their caretaker. The model has an effect on attention, processing of information and making of decisions.

In an ideal situation, the child's attachment figures are supposed to be sensitive and responsive to the child's needs. Sensitive- meaning they are able to assess the child's needs in a given situation and responsive meaning that they have to be able to respond in a manner that is consistent and accurate.

Ainsworth in 1973 however discovered that not all caregivers are responsive.It was discovered that continuous insensitive and unresponsive caretaking leads to a feeling of anxiety in the child leading to anxious internal models of attachment.

There are four different classifications of attachment which can be found in children and they are:

- Secure attachment: A child whose caregiver consistently shows responsiveness and sensitivity tends to rely on their caregivers to take care of their needs for closeness, soothing, emotional support and protection.
- Anxious ambivalent attachment: In a situation whereby the caregiver blows hot and cold, in other words, inconsistently showing responsiveness and sensitivity to the infant, the child tends to not feel reassured when the caregiver returns back
- Anxious attachment behaviour: A caregiver who consistently is unresponsive and insensitive causes the child to completely avoid their caregivers
- Disorganised attachment occurs when there is a complete lack of attachment behaviour.

Bowbly theorized that an anxious unstable attachment is a leading cause of agoraphobia. He uses the separation anxiety which is the fear of living at home as a major symptom of this condition. He believes that the fear is as a result of pattern of studies of human interaction. Some of the patterns include:

- PATTERN A: Mother or in some rare cases father, suffer from anxiety conditions relating to attachment figures

- PATTERN B: The patient fears a possibility of something happening to either mother or father while they are not in a close range of their parents causing the patient to either stay at home or insisting on the parent accompanying the patient whenever a need arises to leave the house.

- PATTERN C: The patient fears that something terrible might happen to the caregiver when they are not around, causing them to remain home to avoid that.

Bowlby considers extreme ambivalence (switch in feelings) as a major feature of parents of children with agoraphobia. The parents who of the children in pattern A-C listed above have the characteristics of overprotectiveness, dominance, narcissism and guilt inducing, and might even be agoraphobic themselves. Threats by parents of suicide, abandonment and separation gives more credence to the disorder.

Recent research shows that children and adolescents who are anxious-ambivalent are seen to be more anxious than their peers or more avoidant in nature.

SPATIAL THEORY

There is a theory that the symptoms of agoraphobia are spatial in nature causing the disorder to be very important in geography. As a result of the studies which prove that agoraphobia affects more women than men, a lot of feminist geographers have put up an argument stating that due to the vulnerability and powerlessness of women, they are more susceptible to agoraphobia. This theory however does not count for all women neither does it explain the male ratio of people suffering from the disorder.

In the opinion of Freud, a fear of going out could represent turning away from desire, imagined as taking the form of unrestrained sexuality. He focused on agoraphobia as an issue affecting mainly women.

This approach tries to decode the symptom as a hidden expression of a deeper connection. This theory is the basis of most feminist explanations for the disorder. Unlike Freud, most see women's vulnerability as an unequal distribution of power not as sexually repressed.

The arguments are that

- Women are conditioned by society to see themselves as weak and vulnerable when compared to men
- Women are at a disadvantage in terms of power, control and influence (crosby, 1994)

According to the argument, in patriarchal societies, women are naturally liable to get agoraphobia. According to Bem, men are commended for behaviours that are assertive, commanding, independent and competent while women are expected to be submissive, passive, fearful and non-assertive. Hence, agoraphobia and panic attacks become typical responses expected of the weaker sex.

Some other scholars use a historical approach to describe the relationship between agoraphobia and women relating agoraphobia to a 19th century opinion of the "hysterical woman".

Using the phenomena of depersonalization and derealization, the agoraphobic person is often described as fragile making the female psyche even more at risk than the male.

SUBSTANCE USE DISORDERS

In most cases, people who struggle with agoraphobia often turn to substance abuse in order to get by and numb the feelings of anxiety. Temporary benefits of alcohol and drug use is the short term relief from anxiety through relaxation.

However, more often than not, the symptoms of agoraphobia increase with drug and illicit substance use.

Drugs and alcohol affect the way signals and chemical messengers are dispersed throughout the brain and the central nervous system..

The presence of central nervous suppressants such as alcohol, opioid and benzodiazepine drugs increases the neurotransmitters such as Dopamine and GABA (Gamma-aminobutyric acid). The benefits of both are that dopamine heightens the level of pleasure while GABA reduces the stress response reducing feelings of anxiety. These substances make a person feel stronger and brave enough to go through situations they were scared of going through before.

However, this only hides the symptoms for a short period of time and its effects afterwards such as depression, hangovers, increased anxiety, physical pain and extreme discomfort are hazardous to the health.

Regular use of alcohol and drugs can result in the brain waves and neurotransmitters being transmitted in less previous way. When the effects of these substances pay out, anxiety returns even more than it was before as a result of the low levels of neurotransmitters and brain waves.

A survey result showed that each year an estimated amount of 20 million Americans aged 12 and above suffer from substance use disorder More than eight million Americans will have multiple substance use disorders alongside mental health disorder.

The negative effects of the substances are listed:

- Alcohol and Agoraphobia:. Taking a little bit of alcohol or any substance with the aim of sleeping or hanging out with friends can be permitted. However, taking those with the aim of suppressing issues such as panic disorder or any other anxiety disorder is not advisable. Studies show an alarming relationship between alcohol and mental health disorders.

Alcohol is a drug that suppresses the central nervous system. At the beginning, alcohol operates just like a sedative and creates a sense of euphoria and reduced inhibition. It also gives the impression that it is providing the relief from agoraphobia caused by the anxiety.

However, the effects of alcohol abuse over the long term are not so pleasant. A chronic case of alcohol abuse could lead to tolerance, dependency and further damage to a lot of organs of the body including the brain, heart and liver.

For many people who are suffering from agoraphobia, the alcohol becomes a crutch in situations which cause for social interactions. The problem with this however is the tolerance that slowly builds to the effects of this substance. Thus, leading to an increased amount of alcohol consumed in order to get the effect desired.

- AGORAPHOBIA AND MARIJUANA ABUSE

Marijuana is an addictive substance usually used by people who self medicate to try to relieve and lessen the fear and anxiety which are well-known symptoms of agoraphobia. However, this leads to an increased pulse rate, decreased blood pressure and an extreme case of dizziness and light heartedness.

One of the most dangerous side effects of agoraphobia is the worry and anxiety which increases the symptoms. The need to feel relief again (addiction) is one of the main disadvantages of marijuana abuse

- STIMULANTS AND AGORAPHOBIA

Drugs which are known as stimulant drugs awaken the central nervous system, releasing stress response thus increasing the levels of stress and anxiety in the body. Some of the symptoms which are thus experienced are elevated heartbeat, dizziness and palpitations all of which can cause anxiety making the dreadful symptoms of agoraphobia even worse.

Stimulants are able to create permanent changes in the way the nerve cells of the brain communicate and after emulation regulation. When the stimulants finally leave, there will be a drop in the neurotransmitter levels hence increasing the symptoms of panic and anxiety

Excessive use of tranquilizers and sleeping pills are linked to the initial phase of agoraphobia. Tobacco smoking was also associated with the creation and emergence of agoraphobia with panic disorder attached to it. While researchers have not been able to pinpoint the direct constituent of tobacco that results in anxiety-panic with or without the symptoms of agoraphobia

- EVOLUTIONARY PSYCHOLOGY

Research into the vast world of emotions began what was discovered that emotions mean a lot more than just feelings but are associated with physiological and behavioural changes that make up a huge part of emotions. This has led to the view of emotions being experienced at three different levels namely:

- mental or psychological level,
- the physiological and neuro level
- Behavioural level

These three levels are present even in some of the emotions even one as simple as fear. Ethologically, some of the symptoms exhibited in the throes of a panic attack is seen as an adaptation to aid flight from life-threatening danger. The sudden increase in the speed and strength of the cardiac contractile muscles send extra blood to the muscles while the gut feels empty and skin loses its color because blood is shunted somewhere else. Quickened breathing alongside taking deep breaths increases blood oxygen level.

There is an intense mental activity with the aim of finding possible escape routes. When the urge to flee is taken into action, a lot of effort is put into escape.

The direction of flight is usually to the home and family of a trust kin which is similar to animals that rely on their skin for protection and sense of safety.

Agoraphobic patients do not develop a fear of the specific object of attention at the moment of panic but rather, the general environment where this panic attack occurred. Furthermore, certain situations which were associated with increased risk of danger during primate evolution may have gained the capacity to reduce the panic threshold. Places could include an open landscape without trees which offers no safe refuge, a closed in space which increases the risk of being trapped in.

Women might benefit in such situations more than men from a low panic threshold and a likelihood to avoid going to far places because they are less able to defend themselves as compared to men. Other reasons could include difficulty in flight with children attached to them, and also because food gathering relatively doesn't require as long an excursion as does hunting.

According to this theory, many phobias are simply prepared fears. This leads people with such prepared fears to have a survival advantage. Repeated experience of fear causing situations is a basic trigger for avoidance.

SYMPTOMS

The severity of agoraphobia in different individuals varies. A person with a severe case of the disorder might find themselves chained to the house and unable to go out but someone with mild to moderate severity of the disorder might be able to transit short distances/

Agoraphobia symptoms are classified into 3 major categories. These include:

- Physical symptoms
- Cognitive symptoms
- Behavioural symptoms

PHYSICAL SYMPTOMS

The physical symptom only occurs when you are in a location or environment that triggers their anxiousness. Due to their panic attacks, many patients suffering from avoid situations that could potentially lead to triggers,

The physical symptoms of agoraphobia Is similar to the symptoms experienced during a panic attack. Some of the symptoms include:

- Quickened heartbeat
- Quickened breathing (hyperventilating)
- Hot and sweaty feeling
- Sudden sick feeling
- Chest pain
- Dysphagia which means to have a problem swallowing
- Diarrhea

- Trembling of the body
- Sudden ringing in the ears (tinnitus)
- Faint feeling

COGNITIVE SYMPTOMS

These symptoms can be independent of the physical symptoms. In other words, these symptoms can be but are not always related to physical symptoms

These symptoms could include one or more of the following:

- The fear that a panic attack will occur in public leaving us embarrassed or feeling stupid in front of other people
- The fear that a panic attack will be life threatening. The fear of death will be foremost In your mind, thoughts of not being able to breathe and heart stopping
- The fear of being stuck and unable to escape when the panic attack arises.
- The niggling fear that you are losing your sanity
- The fear of publicly losing control
- The fear of ruining your reputation by publicly breaking out into a trembling fit

- The fear of being made fun of

Some other related psychological symptoms which are not all related to panic attacks are:

- A niggling thought of being unable to properly work or function without the aid of people
- Some other people are scared of being alone in their house. They are filled with anxiety for both themselves and people around them. This Is called monophobia
- A general feeling of anxiety and fear

BEHAVIOURAL SYMPTOMS

These symptoms are more often than not related to behavior. Examples of such agoraphobic symptoms include:

- Avoiding environments and situations that could lead to panic attacks arising. Examples of such environments could include crowded spaces, markets, public spaces or queues.
- Not being able to step out of the house for so long.
- Being attached to someone who is your safe space before being able to step out.
- Not being able to step far away from your designated safe space.

Even though some people are still able to do some of those things, they still feel extreme fear and anxiety even when doing so.

REFERENCE

1. Bouton, M.E., Mineka, S., & Barlow, D.H. (2001). A modern learning theory perspective on the etiology of panic disorder. Psychological Review, 108, 4-32.

2. Mathews, A.M., Gelder, M.G., & Johnston, D.W. (1981). Agoraphobia – nature and treatment. The Guilford Press, New York.

3. Michelson, L., & Mavissakalian, M. (1983). Temporal stability of self-report measures in agoraphobia research. Behaviour Research and Therapy, 21, 695-698.

4. Öst, L.-G. (1990). The Agoraphobia Scale: An evaluation of its reliability and validity. Behaviour Research and Therapy, 27, 123-130.

5. Wittchen, H.-U. & Essau, C.A. (1991). The epidemiology of panic attacks, panic disorder, and agoraphobia. In J.R. Walker, G.R. Norton & C.A. Ross (eds.) Panic Disorder and Agoraphobia

   – A Comprehensive Guide for the Practitioner. Belmont: Brooks/Cole.

CHAPTER FOUR

Lizzie, a young teacher of 25 had just dropped her niece at a daycare when she had her first ever panic attack. She was heading off to school and hadn't even gone very far when she began to feel really dizzy.

Never having experienced the kind of feelings she was experiencing, she tried to calm herself while sifting through what little medical memories she had, trying to find a plausible explanation for what she was feeling. Her conclusion was that she was having a heart attack.

She tried counting her steps as she walked in a bid to calm herself but as she walked, the feeling in her body grew worse.

Her legs began to buckle, her mind began to race, she couldn't breathe, and there was a sudden need inside her to scream for help.

Sitting down on a nearby chair she found, she tried to quell the panic she was feeling inside of her. Trying to rest, she found that she couldn't. She was completely panic stricken. Her arms and her legs were shaking, her tongue felt swollen and she found it difficult to even say a word. People were starting to look at her strangely, it wasn't always you see a woman who looked like she was on the brink of death.

The worst thing about these panic attacks were that they didn't even stop,. She kept trying to see if they would happen again, and they kept on repeating themselves-she felt cursed.

She went to the doctor and he gave her phenobarbitone for depression. In her words, she couldn't tell him about the incident because she felt he was going to think she was stupid and tell her the attacks were all in her head.

But after a while, as the panic kept on recurring, she finally gave in and told him about the symptoms. Not really understanding what she was going through, he pumped her with more and more anti-depression pills until she felt as if she was running mad.

The more she swallowed more pills, the more anxious she felt. She started getting these attacks in shops, in malls, at the post office- she literally had them everywhere.

It had become a cycle. She would go to a store and feel the beginning of a panic attack rising. Feeling anxious, she had pick everything in sight on the counter not even bothering to look at what it was then run to the queue, frantically praying the queue would move along quickly. The worst thing was not even being able to step outside and walk leisurely, she had to run or walk fast else she would have a nervous breakdown right there in front of whatever shop she was in.

The worst blow for her was the lack of understanding from her family. It seemed like everyone she met told her to get over it, and that it was all in her head. Her social life had disintegrated as she couldn't explain what she was going through with anyone in her circle of friends. She had to take a break from doing a job she really loved and that broke her heart even further.

After ten months, the doctor finally got tired of regularly seeing her at his office and referred her to a psychiatrist. In a way, this felt like the full confirmation from him that she had finally gone mad.

A lot of panic attacks and pep talks later, she finally found herself shuffling towards the psychiatrist office where a lot of tests and routine examination were conducted and she finally had the name of her condition spelt out - Agoraphobia

ASSESSMENT OF AGORAPHOBIA

Before the diagnosis of panic disorder or agoraphobia, the general practitioner has to rule out any possible medical condition which might be responsible for the bodily sensations feared by the patient. An example of this could be panic like sensations caused by thyroid and vestibular problems.

The doctor should also ensure that the physical symptoms which are associated with the patient's agoraphobia are not as a result of substance imbibing. If psychoactive substances are used by the patient, the doctor has to carefully assess the time the patient began experiencing the physiological effects of the substance. This is to determine if the sensations experienced by the patient are caused by substance.

A clinician must also assess if the avoidance behavior of the patient is not better accounted for by the DSM-IV diagnosis. It could be as a misdiagnosed case of panic disorder, special phobia and generalised anxiety, some of whose symptoms are often mistaken as symptoms of agoraphobia.

Usually, agoraphobia is often detected at the first interview meant for diagnosis. A certain interview format developed by the DIS and the World Health Organization have been developed but this doesn't always yield true diagnosis.

Good diagnosis is usually obtained with a doctor who interviews the patient in a bid to explore the differential diagnosis fully. One of the supported interviews called the "Anxiety Disorder Schedule Interview" for DSM-IV prepares a semi-structured format which the doctor uses to understand and assess the function of some of the reported symptoms of anxiety and avoidance behaviour. The information obtained allows the doctor to conduct an analysis of the individuals ideologic conditions, and the avoidance technique of that individual/patient.

DIAGNOSIS OF AGORAPHOBIA

DIFFERENTIAL DIAGNOSIS

This process involves using diagnostic procedures used by physicians and doctors to distinguish between diseases and conditions from others with similar clinical properties. Its main aim is to diagnose the specific condition or disease of a patient.

1. Avoidance: The two factor theory postulated by Mowrer in 1947 views anxiety as more than learned aversiveness. The theory highlights capabilities to control, reduce, eliminate escape or avoid threatening situations as one of the key factors of anxiety disorders. A research in 1986 by Rachman states that people who were less avoidant had more anxiety disorders as compared to those who were more avoidant. The results of the experiment showed that physical restraint increases the level of aggravation and increased sympathetic activation.

Ina bid to manipulate avoidance levels, some subjects were asked to reduce their aversive emotional state caused by the addition of 20% CO_2 into their air as compared to those who were ordered to sit and not interfere.

The experiment showed that people with increased emotional avoidance, were more anxious and aversive to the task.

2. SPECIFIC PHOBIA: A specific phobia is a type of anxiety disorder with an utmost fear of a specific situation or object. While everybody worries about doing something, this fear affects the life and personal relationships of the person suffering from the disorder.

These fear occurs when a person is faced with the situation and often find that there is little to no avoiding the fear even after the situation can't handle the fear.

The main difference between specific phobia and agoraphobia is that the former is centered on harm caused by the situation or object while the latter is caused by the availability of escape routes or people who might help in the case of an attack.

3. SOCIAL ANXIETY DISORDER: This is an anxiety disorder identified by a strong fear of social and public situations which could cause them extreme humiliation.

People who are afraid of only one type of social situation or just a few of them are called non-generalized specific social phobia. There is no specific route in which social anxiety disorder came about. For some, it was moving into a new place or a change in occupation. Even being booed off the stage can cause a slow descent into the social anxiety phobia.

The worst thing about being socially scared is the knowledge that their fear is overrated and easy to counter leading them to feel less anxious and more insecure about themselves.

4. PANIC DISORDER: Panic disorder is a condition in which the person suffering from that condition has continuous panic attacks. Panic disorder is often quite difficult to differentiate from other anxiety disorders, namely depression and other mental illnesses.

The symptoms of panic attacks which makes it different from general anxiety are the length of episodes which last for an unspecified amount of time often discrete and the more intense symptoms people suffer from.

It is not evident as to why some people experience agoraphobia after their first panic attack and others do not.

There is an increased rate of depression in individuals with panic disorders. Increased alcohol consumption, alcohol or illicit drugs are often used in an attempt to stop attacks

Even if all the criteria relating to panic disorder are met, agoraphobia can still not be diagnosed unless there is a constant of avoidance behaviours alongside panic attacks extending to two separate situations.

5. SEPARATION ANXIETY DISORDER: This is an anxiety disorder in which a person suffers from a huge amount of anxiety on issues relating to separation from home or people whom the individual has formed strong emotional ties to. This person could either be a sibling, friend, parent, etc.

It is increasingly common in children between the age of six and seven months to three years, although it might arise in children older than that.

The difference between this disorder and agoraphobia is the fear. Fear in separation anxiety disorder is centered on detachment from a loved one meanwhile in agoraphobia, the fear is centered on environment and situations that results in anxiety and avoidance.

6. POST-TRAUMATIC STRESS DISORDER: This is a mental disorder which might develop if a person is exposed to traumatizing Events such as assault, warfare, traffic accidents, abuse as a child or any other militating events that might have had a negative effect on one's life.

Some symptoms could include terrifying thoughts and dreams relating to the incident, mental or physical distress to traumatic cues and fight or flight syndrome.

The difference between post traumatic stress disorder, and agoraphobia is the limit of avoidance behaviours. In post traumatic disorders, the limit of the avoidance behaviors extend to situations reminding the individual of the traumatic experience faced. Meanwhile, in agoraphobia, the avoidance behavior extends to a range of situations which have no relationship to any trauma.

7. MAJOR DEPRESSIVE DISORDER: This is also known as depression. It is a mental disorder which is characterized by at least two weeks of low mood and aversion to activity.

Symptoms related to this disorder includes a reduced self esteem, and an accompanying loss of interest in activities which the person normally found available. Other symptoms include low energy and pain without an underlying cause.

Individuals with this disorder may become very isolated not leaving the house. In agoraphobia., the avoidance behavior is as a result of fear of available means of escape or help will be available if panic symptoms develop or if the individual loses control.

DIAGNOSIS

According to the Diagnostic and Statistical Manual of Mental Disorders (DSM) in DSM-III showed a change in the relationship between agoraphobia and panic.

A major change found in DSM-5 was the separation of panic disorder and agoraphobia and additional specifications were added to differentiate between agoraphobia and other types of disorders. The situations and environments are avoided because of the scary belief that escape becomes impossible or that help becomes unavailable in the event of a loss of control.

The diagnostic specifications for DSM-5 for Agoraphobia include the following:

- Extreme fear or worry caused by exposure to some of the situations:
  - Using public transport

- Being in areas that are open

- Being in areas that are closed

- Standing in queues or in the midst of a crowd

- Standing alone away from the house

- He or she avoids the situations listed above because of fear of becoming stuck or unavailability of help in the eventuality of a panic attack
- The situations listed above cause fear and anxiousness
- The situations listed above are avoided and more often than not, help from the loved ones are required or tolerated with strong fear
- The fear of the person is extreme when compared to the possibility of the dangerous situation
- The fear and avoidance is continuous and usually lasts for about 6 months on average.
- The fear and avoidance experienced by the individual causes them extreme distress
- Even in the presence of another medical condition alongside the disorder, the fear or avoidance is high

- The fear and avoidance experienced by the individual is not better explained by the symptoms of other disorders.

CHAPTER FIVE

TREATMENT OF AGORAPHOBIA

Damien, a 30 year old African- American male was a single father of a four year old daughter. Ever since the birth of his daughter and the death of his wife a week after, he has been plagued with anxiety and panic attacks.

According to Damien, the first time he experienced was when he got the news of his wife's death. He was driving home with his new daughter sleeping behind in the car seat when he started feeling detached. It suddenly felt like everything began moving in slow motion, as if his was the only car moving and the rest were on a standstill.

Luckily, he was able to drive back home without an accident. However,a few days later, the same thing happened on his way to the grocery store. He suddenly started hyperventilating and feeling sick. Taking a sip of the water he discovered he couldn't swallow. He describes this as one of the scariest situations of his life This experience scared him so much that he decided to limit his business activities to the house.

However, when reading one day, he stumbled upon the term Agoraphobia which sounded similar to the symptoms he was facing. Booking an appointment with a therapist after lots of self-talk

On arrival to the hospital, he was directed to the therapist's office where he was asked a couple of questions and asked to undergo a series of tests. His suspicions were correct and his diagnosis came out as he expected. He was then placed on a series of treatments to correct the disorder.

HISTORY OF AGORAPHOBIA TREATMENT

FIRST GENERATION STUDIES

Over 50 years ago, the first research reports on the treatment of agoraphobia appeared. The first generation studies had some features in common with each other. One of the main features was their foundation on DSM-III and the other being the focus on these sets on situational avoidance rather than reduction of panic attacks. The element of these first generation treatments involved having the patient confront the panic-inducing element with the aim of helping them overcome the panic attacks and avoidance they felt. Some of these treatments include:

- GRADED RETRAINING:

In 1963, Meyer and Gelder stated that phobic symptoms seemed to be good for behaviour therapy; usually seen in clinics and difficult to be treated using other means. In this method of treatment, patients were urged to relax and with the aid of a therapist exposed to fear-inducing real life situations while striving to maintain a calm and relaxed state.

The major downsides of this form of treatment was

its extremely disappointing results after a long time wasted. One of the major critics of this form of treatment was Eysenck whose main criticism was their use of this method rather than the desensitization method which he termed a better therapy technique.

- SYSTEMATIC DESENSITIZATION METHOD

The main focus of this method is to teach the patient to produce inhibitory physiological responses (teaching them the act of deep muscle relaxation)in order to limit the anxiety response to extremely terrifying situations. When treating 20 patients with agoraphobia, Gelder and Marks compared desensitization with the attention placebo control.

Gelder, Marks and Wolff in 1967 discovered that systematic desensitization was a bit more effective than individual or group psychotherapy, reducing the symptoms of phobia in 14 patients with agoraphobia. Wolff also pointed out that desensitization isn't functional except in those with a specific fear of open space.

IMAGINAL FLOODING

This involves exposing the patient to high levels of feared situations for a longer period of time. Watson, Gaind and Marks in 1971 reported reductions in symptoms of phobia after measurement of clinical ratings and heart rate response to phobic imagery among 10 agoraphobics.

Other research has been conducted to compare the process of imaginal flooding with that of desensitization. One of the research studies by Boulougouris et al. in the year 1971 showed that the process of imaginal flooding did better significantly when compared to desensitization.

In a bid to further examine the effect of anxiety experienced during flooding and its role during the flooding process, four scientists Chambless, Foa, Groves, and Goldstein in the year 1971 performed an experiment comparing imaginal flooding alone, imaginal flooding plus a relaxant drug and a control group with 27 outpatient agoraphobics. The results proved that imaginal flooding reduced phobic symptoms. A hypothesis stating that patients who experienced higher amount of anxiety during the period of treatment benefited more from the treatment.

SELF OBSERVATION

Between the years 1974 and 1975, a new treatment procedure was introduced by Emmelkamo and his colleagues. This method encourages patients to slowly enter feared situations and if there is a challenge of undue anxiety, the patient is cautioned to withdraw and return immediately. This procedure is repeated for a number of trials over a period of time with each trial session being 90 minutes approximately. The difference between this and the other methods is the absence of social reinforcement by the therapist.The patients are given a stopwatch and asked to record their time spent outside, In this method, the patients are not undergo a lessening of anxiety before ending the trial.

In 1974, Emmelkamp did research comparing the effectiveness of self-observation, flooding, a combination of both self-observation and flooding and a control containing 20 outpatient agoraphobics. Patient in the first three groups received twelve sessions of about 90 minutes each over a four week period. Patients in the category for flooding went through 45 minutes of flooding in imagination treatment followed immediately by 45 minutes of in vivo flooding in vivo flooding. Patients in the combined group of both flooding and observation treatment went through flooding during the first three sessions and self observation for the remaining sessions.

Even though no major difference was found between flooding and observation, research results showed that there was a major improvement in all three patients in all the categories when phobic anxiety and avoidance were measured. However, the combined treatment of flooding and self observation showed more improvement when compared to the other groups of treatment.

Three people named Everaerd, Rijken, and Emmelkamp in the year 1973 compared approximation and self observation using an experiment with 16 agoraphobic outpatients. In both conditions, patients receive six 90 minutes sessions over a period of three weeks. Results also show there was an improvement in measure of phobic anxiety and in vivo measurement.

PARTICIPANT MODELING/GUIDED MASTERY

This method was first introduced by Bandura and his colleagues using experiments involving cognitive change mechanisms responsible for fear. Similar to the other methods, the patient is exposed to the source of fear. However, in this method, the therapist has an active role to play using some specific mastery enhancing strategies to help the patient fight against their fear.

Some of the strategies include:

- Modeling coping situations by the therapist

- Introduction and fading of performance aids (the therapist sits in a situation where the phobic patient feels at their worst, and gradually fades themselves)

- Setting goals and mastering tasks to help the patient manage tasks which are challenging to the patient. An example of this could be making the patient drive through one exit instead of multiple drive throughs

- Identifying and correcting defensive tactics (getting the patient to loosen their grip on the steering wheel)

- Getting the patient to try out different situations

The first study on guided mastery was performed in 1984 by William, Doseman and Kleifield. Thirty two patients suffering from severe height and phobia for driving were randomly placed in one of the following groups of treatment (I) Guided mastery alone (II) in vivo exposure alone (III) No treatment control. When the results were collated, it was found that people in the group of no treatment control did not show any difference in avoidance behaviors and fear measurements. Guided mastery treatment however showed a greater level of improvement than those receiving in vivo treatment alone when anxiety, behavior and coping levels were measured.

IN VIVO EXPOSURE

This method was postulated by Agras, Leitenberg and Barlow in 1968. This method involved using social encouragement and praise as an incentive for the patients to expose themselves to scary situations. Agoraphobics were encouraged to walk from the clinic to a really busy area downtown . The intervention by the therapist constituted verbal encouragement as an incentive. This was given based on the person's ability to walk further down the road.

This method encouraged the patients to move further and make efforts to complete the task.

At the beginning, it was thought that the praise was the cause of the improvement however later research showed that the patients were already improving right from the beginning and the intervention didn't affect the course of events.

Similar to other exposure techniques, it is directed at real life situations but unlike the grading retraining and desensitization methods, its aim was not for anxiety to be kept at a reduced level

SELF DIRECTED EXPOSURE

For about forty decades approximately, anxiety disorder specialists have suspected that exposure to environments and situations is the major ingredient needed for the successful treatment of agoraphobia. In the advent of this being confirmed as true, many patients would achieve a whole lot more success on their own by entering feared situations with guidance from a therapist, family members or self-help instructor.

SECOND GENERATION TREATMENT STUDIES

In this method, the patients were randomly assigned to a psychological treatment which was compared to another treatment which is usually non-specific in nature.

The studies in these treatment groups have the tendency of being superior to those in the first generation as a result of their

(I) large sample size

(II) use of structured interviews with the intended

purpose of diagnosis to ensure patients meet the agoraphobia threshold

(III) Use of outcome measures which have been psychometrically measured

(IV) Better attention to issues of treatment fidelity

(V) More attention paid to the effect of the treatment on the patient.

The treatments used in this generation of studies tend to be exposure based treatments or treatments required to benefits the exposure based treatments

THIRD GENERATION TREATMENT STUDIES

In this treatment, the patients met DSM-III and DSM-IV criteria to panic disorder with agoraphobia.These method of treatments focus primarily on therapeutic elements which mainly target panic attacks and anxiousness as a result of panic attacks. Three major treatments researched in this generation include

- Cognitive behavioral therapy with a focus on panic
- Cognitive therapy
- Applied relaxation therapy

STUDIES ON DIFFERENT EXPOSURE PARAMETERS ON THE TREATMENT OF AGORAPHOBIA

Since the exposure therapy was found to be quite effective, it is no wonder that different studies were conducted on the different levels of exposure to determine which one was more effective. This section reviews different studies which have shown several distinct parameters of exposure therapy.

- MASSED VS SPACED EXPOSURE SESSIONS

In a bid to understand the exposure therapy methods more and to determine the frequency and duration of sessions to make them more effective, four scientists Foa, Jameson, Turner and Payne in the year 1980 design used a crossover design to compare ten daily sessions and ten weekly sessions in a specific sample of eleven agoraphobic patients comparing their effects. At the end of this experiment, it was determined that the daily sessions outperformed the sessions which was spaced weekly using specific measures of phobia and anxiety.

In the year 1990, another study was designed by Chamless to compare massed versus spaced method of exposure treatment. Nineteen agoraphobic patients received treatments of ten daily or ten weekly sessions of in vivo exposure exposure alongside other strategies such as respiratory control training, stopping of thought, and paradoxical condition with the aim of controlling anxiety level. There was no exposure homework given because of the advantage it gives patients assigned to spaced conditions. There was no significant change observed at either the posttreatment or 6-month follow up. There was also no proof whatsoever to support the claim by previous scientists that massed sessions led to more dropouts and a higher rates of relapse as compared to spaced sessions. Howevwe,the reason why there was a failure finding differences could be as a result of insufficient samples and statistical power.

- BRIEF VERSUS STANDARD TREATMENTS FOR AGORAPHOBIA

The advantage of shortened treatment length over its longer counterparts is lower treatment costs and increased accessibility of care. These advantages are only valid if the treatments for panic disorder with agoraphobia can be shortened without a reduction in effectiveness of treatment.

There is evidence now showing that brief exposure treatments show therapeutic effect on patients when compared to control conditions. Studies also showed that brief lengths of treatments are also as effective as the standard length of treatments.

In the year 1987, a research was conducted by Goisman et al. to determine the effect of shortened exposure treatments on agoraphobic patients. He randomly assigned patients

With agoraphobia, about forty of them to receive exposure instructions from self-exposure treatments from a psychiatrist, self-help help booklet or a computer. Each of these groups showed a tremendous and continuous improvement even after a 6 month follow up.

These results prove that providing exposure instructions regarding the delivery form, affords major therapeutic benefits.

- GROUP VERSUS INDIVIDUALLY ADMINISTERED TREATMENT

Though there has been several researches done on

the effectiveness of group behavioural treatments of agoraphobia, there have been a few studies conducted a head to head comparison of individual and group treatment of agoraphobia.

This research was conducted by Sharp, Power and Swanson in 2004. They compared group based exposure with individual exposure treatments using 97 patients who met DSM-IV criteria for panic disorder with or without agoraphobia. Using the outcome of treatments on patients with agoraphobia, and those showing signs of panic disorder without agoraphobia, there was a symptom reduction in both groups. After 3 months follow up.,40% of the patients receiving group exposure treatments and 58% of the patients receiving individual exposure significantly showed signs of improvement.

Some key notes of this experiment are that 47% of the participants of the study dropped out of the study which is about four times higher than those observed in previous group administered exposure treatments.

THERAPIST ASSISTED VS SELF DIRECTED EXPOSURE

One of the questions commonly asked in the treatments of patients with agoraphobia is the question of if the presence of a therapist has greater advantage over therapist unaccompanied exposure.

The reasons why people believe that the presence of a therapist who offers instructions, guidance and moral support and also solve problems encountered during in vivo exposures during treatment might prove beneficial. Not enough data has spoken about the issue although recently, there has been a recent study using an eight-site trial that addresses the effect of therapy assistance using in vivo exposure.

In this experiment, 369 patients who met the DSM-IV criteria for moderate to severe levels of agoraphobia were placed at random in different control groups or to different exposure groups in which they either (i) did all situational confrontations as homework (ii) had a therapist present for a third of all situations. In this group, the therapist accompanied the patient on one in vivo exposure and then gave the patient the remaining two confrontations as homework

The research shows that while both exposure treatment groups showed positive results, those who received therapy assisted in vivo exposure treatments showed better results especially in situational avoidance.

TREATMENT STRATEGIES

Asides from treatment strategies commonly used during history, additional strategies have been postulated with somewhat confusing results

- Assertiveness Training

Agoraphobic patients are often described as people who suffer from low assertiveness and are really dependent. This has provided a rationale for replacing exposure treatments with assertiveness training. In 1983, Emmelkamp discovered that while the exposure treatment showed greater results especially when it came to phobic resistance, assertiveness training produced improvements in levels of assertiveness than exposure. Assertiveness training was thus found to be more specific, having no great impact on the general symptoms of agoraphobia.

- Relaxation:

In 1986, Michelson compared the addition of a therapist-assisted exposure, self-contradictory intention and deep muscle relaxation to instructions for self-directed exposure in vivo. This study provided aid for the hypothesis that treatment which was in harmony with the patients' pretreatment syndrome yielded better results.

- Cognitive therapy:

These strategies are common in the treatment of panic disorder with agoraphobia. The use of his technique was rationalised during the early stages as having a purely beneficial purpose. However, this theory has been replaced by the belief that the effectiveness of cognitive therapy for panic attacks could also be expected to have a similar effect on the treatment of panic disorder with agoraphobia.

Early studies do not provide training or support for self-teaching training or coping techniques. Those earlier studies used in cognitive therapy are considered to be crude varieties of cognitive therapy strategies using today's standards. However, the cognitive therapy methods were closely linked to treatment directly focused on panic attacks.

In 1994, Hout, Arntz and Hoekstra took an interest in the different effects of cognitive therapy and exposure. Two groups of subjects were compared- one group receiving four sessions of cognitive therapy followed by eight sessions, where the cognitive therapy treatment was combined with exposure. The other group received four sessions of a non-specific associative therapy followed by eight sessions in vivo. The results showed that cognitive therapy reduce panic attacks greatly but had little to no effect on agoraphobia. Exposure therapy however had a great effect on agoraphobia but didn't have any effect on agoraphobia.

In 1996, Williams and Falbo compared eight sessions of cognitive therapy, mastery therapy or the combination of both. The results showed that while all treatments showed change, 3 out of 9 patients in the guided mastery therapy showed evidence of higher change score rates than cognitive therapy.

Another research done by Bouchard in 1995 compared cognitive therapy to exposure in vivo plus interoceptive exposure. Treatment was provided in small groups and was done with specific recommendations unlike exposure therapy which involved repetition and prolonging of some of the exercises. The conclusion of the authors was that while each of the tests did equally well in the individual based measures, high end functioning at post test was achieved by 86% of exposure patients as compared to the 64% of cognitive therapy patients.

RESPIRATORY RETRAINING

Hyperventilation has often been discussed both in terms of possible causes and as a basis for possible treatment options in panic disorder. Breathing has been postulated as a means attempting to get anxiety under control and a means of exposure.

In a research done in 1984, Bonn, Readhead andTimmons noted an improvement in the long term response of patients treated with breathing retraining method before exposure. Teaching slow diaphragmatic breathing as a coping technique has become a major feature in most psychological treatments. However, when breathing retraining was added to cognitive behavioural training for panic disorder with or without agoraphobia, it didn't add any clear benefits and the results even suggested that it might have led to a less than complete recovery or possible relapse.

In another study by Hibbert and Chan in the year 1989, patients with panic and agoraphobia were divided into groups with the first group receiving 2 sessions of breathing retraining followed by three weekly sessions of in vivo exposure treatment while the second group received two weeks of supportive therapy followed by three weekly sessions of in vivo exposure therapy with no breathing treatment. At the end of the treatment, patients receiving breathing retraining showed greater improvements.

When joined together, these results provide little to no proof that breathing therapy enhances the efficiency of either combined therapy treatment or exposure interventions for panic disorder with agoraphobia.

PSYCHODYNAMIC TREATMENT APPROACHES

This therapy method has been tested as a possible method for the treatment of agoraphobia. This approach is based on the belief that conflicts from childhood activated by adult stressors have a major role in the cause of agoraphobia.

The main aim of this method is to help the patient gain control by addressing suppressed inner conflicts, led by experiences that come up during exposure.

In 1990, Hoffart and Manisen compared the effectiveness of psychodynamic therapy alone with another program that fused both exposure therapy and psychodynamic therapy administered to a sample of agoraphobic patients. After a year follow up, the results showed a greater improvements in patients with the integrated psychodynamic and exposure treatment groups based on their abilities to handle scary situations alone. While the group treated with psychodynamic therapy alone showed improvement, it was not maintained during the one year follow up.

The results of this study showed that psychodynamic treatment approach alone has little long –term therapeutic benefit while the psychodynamic and exposure therapy has great improvement.

INTERPERSONAL PSYCHOTHERAPY

When presented with data suggesting that interpersonal stressors was one of the causative factors leading to the onset of panic and agoraphobia, it is expected that psychotherapy aimed at correcting those problems could benefit patients with agoraphobia.

Interpersonal psychotherapy is a time based, structured treatment which was originally developed with the aim of treating depression. It has been adapted to be effective in the treatment of some problems including bulimia, major depression, bipolar disorder and substance use disorders.

A research done by Vos, Huibers, Del and Arntz in the year 2012 compared the psychotherapy technique with the cognitive behaviour treatment using a sample of 91 patients who met the DSM-IV criteria for panic disorder with moderate to severe agoraphobia.

The protocol used in IPT were (i) grouping panic disorder in terms of the medical model (ii) determine the focus of treatment (iii) exploring and improvement of different intrapersonal problems (iv) Treatment termination.

However, the results obtained showed that CBT produced greater improvement in the frequency of panic attack and measures of agoraphobia. This showed that the IPT technique isn't really significant in the treatment of moderate to severe agoraphobia.

ACCEPTANCE AND COMMITMENT THERAPY

This technique was designed with the aim of promoting a balance of acceptance and change unlike the other treatment methods which had the goals of treatment as correcting maladaptive behaviour.

This method suggests that patients should accept the experience of behaviours and emotions without judgement and commit to behave in a way which is similar to their values. However, this treatment method is still in the beginning stages with only a limited amount of case studies available.

A case study of this method of treatment is the case of Carrascoso Lopez in 2000 who was diagnosed with panic disorder with agoraphobia treated with ACT. Though the therapy incorporated techniques from the CBT method of treatment, such as in vivo exercises and exposure, the techniques were adjusted to be in alignment with the ACT goals which was to learn to abandon all attempts to control body sensations and strive to reduce the fear response to those sensations.

Results showed a significant decrease in symptoms of panic and agoraphobia alongside reduction of behaviours of escape and avoidance.

Four scientists Codd, Twohig, Crosby and Enno in the year 2011 reported the outcome of another case in which agoraphobia was treated using the ACT method. In this case however, in-session exposure therapy methods were avoided in a bid to reduce the overlap of ACT procedures with other treatment procedures. After the treatment, the patient showed a reduction in agoraphobia symptoms and no longer met the criteria for agoraphobia and panic disorders. an interesting thing to note was that the client's anxiety level remained constant all through the period of the experiment.

This caused the authors to suggest that ACT does not alter the severity of anxiety experienced by the patient, rather, it alters the function of panic and anxiety in the patient.

CHAPTER FIVE

TREATMENT OF AGORAPHOBIA

Damien, a 30 year old African- American male was a single father of a four year old daughter. Ever since the birth of his daughter and the death of his wife a week after, he has been plagued with anxiety and panic attacks.

According to Damien, the first time he experienced was when he got the news of his wife's death. He was driving home with his new daughter in the car seat behind when he started feeling detached. It suddenly felt like everything began moving in slow motion, as if his was the only car moving and the rest were on a standstill.

Luckily, he was able to drive back home without an accident. However, a few days later, the same thing happened on his way to the grocery store. He suddenly experienced started hyperventilating and suddenly started feeling sick. Taking a sip of the water he discovered he couldn't swallow. This scared him more than ever.

This experience scared him so much that he decided to limit his business activities to the house. However, when reading one day, he stumbled upon the term Agoraphobia which sounded similar to the symptoms he was facing. Booking an appointment with a therapist after lots of self-talk

On arrival to the hospital, he was directed to the therapist's office where he was asked a couple of questions and asked to undergo a series of tests. His suspicions were correct and his diagnosis came out as he expected.

He was then placed on a series of treatments to correct the disorder.

HISTORY OF AGORAPHOBIA TREATMENT

FIRST GENERATION STUDIES

Over 50 years ago, the first research reports on the treatment of agoraphobia appeared. The first generation studies had some features in common with each other. One of the main features being their foundation on DSM-III and the other being the focus on these sets on situational avoidance rather than reduction of panic attacks. The element of these first generation treatments involved having the patient confront the panic-inducing element with the aim of helping them overcome the panic attacks and avoidance they felt. Some of these treatments include:

- GRADED RETRAINING:

In 1963, Meyer and Gelder stated that phobic symptoms seemed to be good for behaviour therapy; usually seen in clinics and difficult to be treated using other means. In this method, patients were urged to relax and with the aid of a therapist exposed to fear-inducing real life situations while striving to maintain a calm and relaxed state.

The major downside of this form of treatment was its extremely disappointing results after a long time wasted. One of the major critics of this form of treatment was Eysenck whose main criticism was their use of this method rather than the desensitization method which he termed a better therapy technique.

- SYSTEMATIC DESENSITIZATION METHOD

The main focus of this method is to teach the patient to produce inhibitory physiological responses (teaching them the act of deep muscle relaxation)in order to limit the anxiety response to extremely terrifying situations. When treating 20 patients with agoraphobia, Gelder and Marks compared desensitization with the attention placebo control.

Gelder, Marks and Wolff in 1967 discovered that systematic desensitization was a bit more effective than individual or group psychotherapy, reducing the symptoms of phobia in 14 patients with agoraphobia. Wolff also pointed out that desensitization isn't functional except in those with a specific fear of open space.

IMAGINAL FLOODING

This involves exposing the patient to high level of feared situations for a longer period of time. Watson, Gaind and Marks in 1971 reported reductions in symptoms of phobia after measurement of clinical ratings and heart rate response to phobic imagery among 10 agoraphobics.

Other research has been conducted to compare the process of imaginal flooding with that of desensitization. One of the research studies by Boulougouris et al. in the year 1971 showed that the process of imaginal flooding did better significantly when compared to desensitization.

In a bid to further examine the effect of anxiety experienced during flooding and its role during the flooding process, four scientists Chambless, Foa, Groves, and Goldstein in the year 1971 performed an experiment comparing imaginal flooding alone, imaginal flooding plus a relaxant drug and a control group with 27 outpatient agoraphobics. The results proved that imaginal flooding reduced phobic symptoms. A hypothesis stating that patients who experienced higher amount of anxiety during the period of treatment benefited more from the treatment.

SELF OBSERVATION

Between the years 1974 and 1975, a new treatment procedure was introduced by Emmelkamo and his colleagues. This method encourages patients to slowly enter feared situations and if there is a challenge of undue anxiety, the patient is cautioned to withdraw and return immediately. This procedure is repeated for a number of trials over a period of time with each trial session being 90 minutes approximately. The difference between this and the other methods is the absence of social reinforcement by the therapist.The patients are given a stopwatch and asked to record their time spent outside, In this method, the patients are not undergo a lessening of anxiety before ending the trial.

In 1974, Emmelkamp did research comparing the effectiveness of self-observation, flooding, a combination of both self-observation and flooding and a control containing 20 outpatient agoraphobics. Patient in the first three groups received twelve sessions of about 90 minutes each over a four week period. Patients in the category for flooding went through 45 minutes of flooding in imagination treatment followed immediately by 45 minutes of in vivo flooding in vivo flooding. Patients in the combined group of both flooding and observation treatment went through flooding during the first three sessions and self observation for the remaining sessions.

Even though no major difference was found between flooding and observation, research results showed that there was a major improvement in all three patients in all the categories when phobic anxiety and avoidance were measured. However, the combined treatment of flooding and self observation showed more improvement when compared to the other groups of treatment.

Three people named Everaerd, Rijken, and Emmelkamp in the year 1973 compared approximation and self observation using an experiment with 16 agoraphobic outpatients. In both conditions, patients receive six 90 minutes sessions over a period of three weeks. Results also show there was an improvement in measure of phobic anxiety and in vivo measurement.

PARTICIPANT MODELING/GUIDED MASTERY

This method was first introduced by Bandura and his colleagues using experiments involving cognitive change mechanisms responsible for fear. Similar to the other methods, the patient is exposed to the source of fear. However, In this method, the therapist has an active role to Play using some specific mastery enhancing strategies to help the patient fight against their fear.

Some of the strategies include:

- Modeling coping situations by the therapist
- Introduction and fading of performance aids (the therapist sits in a situation where the phobic patient feels at their worst, and gradually fades themselves)
- Setting goals and mastering tasks to help the patient manage tasks which are challenging to the patient. An example of this could be making the patient drive through one exit instead of multiple drive through
- Identifying and correcting defensive tactics (getting the patient to loosen their grip on the steering wheel)
- Getting the patient to try out different situations

The first study on guided mastery was performed in 1984 by William, Doseman and Kleifield. Thirty two patients suffering from severe height and phobia for driving were randomly placed in one of the following groups of treatment (I) Guided mastery alone (II) in vivo exposure alone (III) No treatment control. When the results were collated, it was found that people in the group of no treatment control did not show any difference in avoidance behaviors and fear measurements. Guided mastery treatment however showed a greater level of improvement than those receiving in vivo treatment alone when anxiety, behavior and coping levels were measured.

IN VIVO EXPOSURE

This method was postulated Agras, Leitenberg and Barlow in 1968. This method involved using social encouragement and praise as an incentive for the patients to expose themselves to scary situations. Agoraphobics were encouraged to walk from the clinic to a really busy area downtown. The intervention by the therapist constituted verbal encouragement as an incentive. This was given based on the person's ability to walk further down the road.

This method encouraged the patients to move further and make efforts to complete the task.

At the beginning, it was thought that the praise was the cause of the improvement however later research showed that the patients were already improving right from the beginning and the intervention didn't affect the course of events.

Similar to other exposure techniques, it is directed at real life situations but unlike the grading retraining and desensitization methods, it was not intended for anxiety to be kept at a reduced level

SELF DIRECTED EXPOSURE

For about forty decades approximately, anxiety disorder specialists have suspected that exposure to environments and situations is the major ingredient needed for the successful treatment of agoraphobia. In the advent of this being confirmed as true, many patients would achieve a whole lot more success on their own by entering feared situations with guidance from a therapist, family members or self-help instructor.

SECOND GENERATION TREATMENT STUDIES

In this method, the patients were randomly assigned to a psychological treatment which was compared to another treatment which is usually non-specific in nature.

The studies in these treatment groups have the tendency of being superior to those in the first generation as a result of their

(I) large sample size

(II) use of structured interviews with the intended purpose of diagnosis to ensure patients meet the agoraphobia threshold

(III) Use of outcome measures which have been psychometrically measured

(IV) Better attention to issues of treatment fidelity

(V) More attention paid to the effect of the treatment on the patient.

The treatments used in this generation of studies tend to be exposure based treatments or treatments required to benefits the exposure based treatments

THIRD GENERATION TREATMENT STUDIES

In this treatment, the patients met DSM-III and DSM-IV criteria to panic disorder with agoraphobia. These method of treatments focus primarily on therapeutic elements which mainly target panic attacks and anxiousness as a result of panic attacks. Three major treatments researched in this generation include

- Cognitive behavioral therapy with a focus on panic
- Cognitive therapy
- Applied relaxation therapy

STUDIES ON DIFFERENT EXPOSURE PARAMETERS ON THE TREATMENT OF AGORAPHOBIA

Since the exposure therapy was found to be quite effective, it is no wonder that different studies were conducted on the different levels of exposure to determine which one was more effective. This section reviews different studies which have shown several distinct parameters of exposure therapy.

MASSED VS SPACED EXPOSURE SESSIONS

In a bid to understand the exposure therapy methods more and to determine the frequency and duration of sessions to make them more effective, four scientists Foa, Jameson, Turner and Payne in the year 1980 design used a crossover design which was counterbalanced to compare ten daily sessions and ten weekly sessions in a specific sample of eleven agoraphobic patients comparing their effects. At the end of this experiment, it was determined that the daily sessions outperformed the sessions which was spaced weekly using specific measures of phobia and anxiety.

In the year 1990, another study was designed by Chamless to compare massed versus spaced method of exposure treatment. Nineteen agoraphobic patients received treatments of ten daily or ten weekly sessions of in vivo exposure exposure alongside other strategies such as respiratory control training, stopping of thought, and paradoxical condition with the aim of controlling anxiety level. There was no exposure homework given because of the advantage it gives patients assigned to spaced conditions. There was no significant change observed at either the post-treatment or 6-month follow up. There was also no proof whatsoever to support the claim by previous scientists that massed sessions led to more dropouts and a higher rate of relapse as compared to spaced sessions. However, the reason why there was a failure finding differences could be as a result of insufficient samples and statistical power.

BRIEF VERSUS STANDARD TREATMENTS FOR AGORAPHOBIA

The advantage of shortened treatment length over its longer counterparts is lower treatment costs and increased accessibility of care. These advantages are only valid if the treatments for panic disorder with agoraphobia can be shortened without a reduction in effectiveness of treatment.

There is evidence now showing that brief exposure treatments show therapeutic effect on patients when compared to control conditions. Studies also showed that brief length of treatments is also as effective as the standard length of treatments.

In the year 1987, a research was conducted by Goisman et al. to determine the effect of shortened exposure treatments on agoraphobic patients. He randomly assigned patients

With agoraphobia, about forty of them to receive exposure instructions from self-exposure treatments from a psychiatrist, self-help help booklet or a computer. Each of these groups showed a tremendous and continuous improvement even after a 6 month follow up.

These results prove that providing exposure instructions regarding the delivery form, affords major therapeutic benefits.

GROUP VERSUS INDIVIDUALLY ADMINISTERED TREATMENT

Though there have been several researches done on the effectiveness of group behavioural treatments of agoraphobia, there have been a few studies conducted a head to head comparison of individual and group treatment of agoraphobia.

This research was conducted by Sharp, Power and Swanson in 2004. They compared group based exposure with individual exposure treatments using 97 patients who met DSM-IV criteria for panic disorder with or without agoraphobia. Using the outcome of treatments on patients with agoraphobia, and those showing signs of panic disorder without agoraphobia, there was a symptom reduction in both groups. After 3 months follow up.,40% of the patients receiving group exposure treatments and 58% of the patients receiving individual exposure significantly showed signs of improvement.

Some key notes of this experiment are that 47% of

the participants of the study dropped out of the study which is about four times higher than those observed in previous group administered exposure treatments.

THERAPIST ASSISTED VS SELF DIRECTED EXPOSURE

One of the questions commonly asked in the treatments of patients with agoraphobia is the question of if the presence of a therapist has greater advantage over therapist unaccompanied exposure.

The reasons why people believe that the presence of a therapist who offers instructions, guidance and moral support and also solve problems encountered during in vivo exposures during treatment might prove beneficial. Not enough data has spoken about the issue although recently, there has been a recent study using an eight-site trial that addresses the effect of therapy assistance using in vivo exposure.

In this experiment, 369 patients who met the DSM-IV criteria for moderate to severe levels of agoraphobia were placed at random in different control groups or to different exposure groups in which they either (i) did all situational confrontations as homework (ii) had a therapist present for a third of all situations. In this group, the therapist accompanied the patient on one in vivo exposure and then gave the patient the remaining two confrontations as homework

The research shows that while both exposure treatment groups showed positive results, those who received therapy assisted in vivo exposure treatments showed better results especially in situational avoidance.

TREATMENT STRATEGIES

Asides from treatment strategies commonly used during history, additional strategies have been postulated with somewhat confusing results

Assertiveness Training

Agoraphobic patients are often described as people who suffer from low assertiveness and are really dependent. This has provided a rationale for replacing exposure treatments with assertiveness training. In 1983, Emmelkamp discovered that while the exposure treatment showed greater results especially when it came to phobic resistance, assertiveness training produced improvements in levels of assertiveness than exposure. Assertiveness training was thus found to be more specific, having no great impact on the general symptoms of agoraphobia.

Relaxation:

In 1986, Michelson compared the addition of a therapist-assisted exposure, self-contradictory intention and deep muscle relaxation to instructions for self-directed exposure in vivo. This study provided aid for the hypothesis that treatment which was in harmony with the patients' pretreatment syndrome yielded better results.

Cognitive therapy:

These strategies are common in the treatment of panic disorder with agoraphobia. The use of his technique was rationalised during the early stages as having a purely beneficial purpose. However, this theory has been replaced by the belief that the effectiveness of cognitive therapy for panic attacks could also be expected to have a similar effect on the treatment of panic disorder with agoraphobia.

Early studies do not provide training or support for self-teaching training or coping techniques. Those earlier studies used in cognitive therapy are considered to be crude varieties of cognitive therapy strategies using today's standards. However, the cognitive therapy methods were closely linked to treatment directly focused on panic attacks.

In 1994, Hout, Arntz and Hoekstra took an interest in the different effects of cognitive therapy and exposure. Two groups of subjects were compared- one group receiving four sessions of cognitive therapy followed by eight sessions, where the cognitive therapy treatment was combined with exposure. The other group received four sessions of a non-specific associative therapy followed by eight sessions in vivo. The results showed that cognitive therapy reduce panic attacks greatly but had little to no effect on agoraphobia. Exposure therapy however had a great effect on agoraphobia but didn't have any effect on agoraphobia.

In 1996, Williams and Falbo compared eight sessions of cognitive therapy, mastery therapy or the combination of both. The results showed that while all treatments showed change, 3 out of 9 patients in the guided mastery therapy showed evidence of higher change score rates than cognitive therapy.

Another research done by Bouchard in 1995

compared cognitive therapy to exposure in vivo plus interoceptive exposure. Treatment was provided in small groups and was done with specific recommendations unlike exposure therapy which involved repetition and prolonging of some of the exercises. The conclusion of the authors was that while each of the tests did equally well in the individual based measures, high end functioning at post test was achieved by 86% of exposure patients as compared to the 64% of cognitive therapy patients.

RESPIRATORY RETRAINING

Hyperventilation has often been discussed both in terms of possible causes and as a basis for possible treatment options in panic disorder. Breathing has been postulated as a means attempting to get anxiety under control and a means of exposure.

In a research done in 1984, Bonn, Readhead andTimmons noted an improvement in the long term response of patients treated with breathing retraining method before exposure. Teaching slow diaphragmatic breathing as a coping technique has become a major feature in most psychological treatments. However, when breathing retraining was added to cognitive behavioural training for panic disorder with or without agoraphobia, it didn't add any clear benefits and the results even suggested that it might have led to a less than complete recovery or possible relapse.

In another study by Hibbert and chan in the year 1989, patients with panic and agoraphobia were divided into groups with the first group receiving 2 sessions of breathing retraining followed by three weekly sessions of in vivo exposure treatment while the second group received two weeks of supportive therapy followed by three weekly sessions of in vivo exposure therapy with no breathing treatment. At the end of the treatment, patients receiving breathing retraining showed greater improvements.

When joined together, these results provide little to no proof that breathing therapy enhances the efficiency of either combined therapy treatment or exposure interventions for panic disorder with agoraphobia.

- PSYCHODYNAMIC TREATMENT APPROACHES

This therapy method has been tested as a possible method for the treatment of agoraphobia. This approach is based on the belief that conflicts from childhood activated by adult stressors have a major role in the cause of agoraphobia.

The main aim of this method is to help the patient

gain control by addressing suppressed inner conflicts, led by experiences that come up during exposure.

In 1990, Hoffart and Manisen compared the effectiveness of psychodynamic therapy alone with another program that fused both exposure therapy and psychodynamic therapy administered to a sample of agoraphobic patients. After a year follow up, the results showed a greater improvements in patients with the integrated psychodynamic and exposure treatment groups based on their abilities to handle scary situations alone. While the group treated with psychodynamic therapy alone showed improvement, it was not maintained during the one year follow up.

The results of this study showed that psychodynamic treatment approach alone has little long –term therapeutic benefit while the psychodynamic and exposure therapy has great improvement.

INTERPERSONAL PSYCHOTHERAPY

When presented with data suggesting that interpersonal stressors was one of the causative factors leading to the onset of panic and agoraphobia, it is expected that psychotherapy aimed at correcting those problems could benefit patients with agoraphobia.

Interpersonal psychotherapy is a time based structured treatment which was originally developed with the aim of treating depression. It has been adapted to be effective in the treatment of some problems including bulimia, major depression, bipolar disorder and substance use disorders.

A research done by Vos, Huibers, Del and Arntz in the year 2012 compared the psychotherapy technique with the cognitive behaviour treatment using a sample of 91 patients who met the DSM-IV criteria for panic disorder with moderate to severe agoraphobia.

The protocol used in IPT were (i) grouping panic disorder in terms of the medical model (ii) determine the focus of treatment (iii) exploring and improvement of different intrapersonal problems (iv) Treatment termination.

However, the results obtained showed that CBT produced greater improvement in the frequency of panic attack and measures of agoraphobia. This showed that the IPT technique isn't really significant in the treatment of moderate to severe agoraphobia.

ACCEPTANCE AND COMMITMENT THERAPY

This technique was designed with the aim of promoting a balance of acceptance and change unlike the other treatment methods which had the goals of treatment as correcting maladaptive behaviour.

This method suggests that patients should accept the experience of behaviours and emotions without judgment and commit to behave in a way which is similar to their values. However, this treatment method is still in the beginning stages with only a limited amount of case studies available.

A case study of this method of treatment is the case of Carrascoso Lopez in 2000 who was diagnosed with panic disorder with agoraphobia treated with ACT. Though the therapy incorporated techniques from the CBT method of treatment, such as in vivo exercises and exposure, the techniques were adjusted to be in alignment with the ACT goals which was to learn to abandon all attempts to control body sensations and strive to reduce the fear response to those sensations.

Results showed a significant decrease in symptoms of panic and agoraphobia alongside reduction of behaviours of escape and avoidance.

Four scientists Codd, Twohig, Crosby and Enno in the year 2011 reported the outcome of another case in which agoraphobia was treated using the ACT method. In this case however, in-session exposure therapy methods were avoided n a bid to reduce the overlap of ACT procedures with other treatment procedures. After the treatment, the patient showed a reduction in agoraphobia symptoms and no longer met the criteria for agoraphobia and panic disorders. an interesting thing to note was that the client's anxiety level remained constant all through the period of the experiment.

This caused the authors to suggest that ACT does not alter the severity of anxiety experienced by the patient; rather, it alters the function of panic and anxiety in the patient.

PHARMACOLOGICAL TREATMENT

Neurological Basis of the Pharmacological Effect

In line with the theory postulated that a dysfunction of brain pathways using γ-aminobutyric acid, serotonin and noradrenaline is one of the pathological causes of panic disorder and agoraphobia, the effectiveness of anti-panic drug is mediated by the effects on the neurochemical systems even though the mechanisms behind this remains unclear.

CHOOSING THE DRUG

Placebo Effect:

This is a well-known occurrence in the treatment of panic disorder (with or without agoraphobia). About 14% to 59% of patients received a panic attack free status after placebo treatment in controlled clinical trials where SSRI, TCA or BDZ were used as active treatment.

This lead to the conclusion that the placebo has a short-term effect on the treatment of panic disorder and agoraphobia. However, the effect disappears with time thus leading to guidelines recommending medication which is more effective than placebo.

Effective Medications:

There are four classes of drugs which are more effective than the placebo and are equally as effective in treating panic disorder and agoraphobia. They are:

- Tricyclic antidepressants (TCA)
- Selective Serotonin reuptake inhibitors (SSRI)
- Monoamine oxidase inhibitors (MAOI)
- High potency Benzodiazepines (BDZ)

SSRI:

Six SSRI are currently available and they include:

- Citalopram
- es-Citalopram
- Fluoxetine
- Paroxetine
- Fluvoxamine
- Sertraline

ADVANTAGE OF SSRI

1. They possess a low affinity for muscarinic, histaminergic and $\propto$-adrenergic and

therefore seldom lead to blurred vision, constipation, dry mouth, increased heart rate, sedation and weight gain.

2. It is safe for severe cardiac effects
3. The risk is lower even after an overdose.

SSRI are not often linked to tolerance and symptoms of withdrawal. SSRIs are often preferred in patients who suffer from obsessive compulsive disorder or other anxiety related disorders. A study done in 2002 of a sample of 43 patients confirmed that the rate of completion of treatment was higher in groups administered with SSRI than with TCA. This led to the conclusion that the higher completion rate was because of the reduced side effects which encouraged participation and completion of drugs.

DISADVANTAGE

SSRIs increase the level of serotonergic activity and causes side effects such as agitation, anxiety, insomnia, nausea, and sexual dysfunction. Since some of these symptoms occur early in treatment before the effect of the drugs start to show, many strategies which could limit these symptoms are taken into consideration.

An abrupt removal of the drug could lead to withdrawal symptoms and some of the symptoms include dizziness, incoordination, headaches, and irritability.

TCA

In 1964, there was a drug used in the treatment of panic disorder called Imipramine and alongside Clomipramine, it was one of the most studied compounds in the treatment of panic disorder and agoraphobia using medications.

ADVANTAGES

It does not offer as many advantages when compared to the SSRI compounds and possesses a whole lot more disadvantages than the aforementioned SSRI compounds.

DISADVANTAGES

The use of TCA is unsafe and less tolerable when compared to the SSRI group. This is because of its antagonistic effect on the muscarinic, histaminergic and α-adrenergic receptors, cardiac rhythm and its detrimental effect when someone overdoses on it in a suicide atempt.

MAOI

Examples of these drugs are phenelzine and tranylcypromine. They are provided for patients who do not respond to other treatments as a result of their extreme side effects especially during a hypertensive crisis. It also leads to dangerous consequences especially when taken with other drugs that increase the level of monoamine and increases the need for dietary restriction. They are considered to be second-line compounds only to be used by experienced therapists.

BENZODIAZEPINES:

These drugs are highly potent and are highly effective in the treatment of panic disorder and agoraphobia. Examples of such drugs include alprazolam, clonazepam and lorazepam.

ADVANTAGES

This drug is still one of the most highly prescribed drugs in the treatment of panic disorder (with or without agoraphobia). It is also one of the only drugs used during a follow up period of ten years in greater than one-third of panic as a treatment medication.

Its onset of action is rapid, the high tolerability and the high patient acceptance are the main reasons why they are so widely used.

DISADVANTAGES

One of the main disadvantages of benzodiazepines is its reduced effectiveness in treating depression associated with panic disorder when compared to TCA or

SSRI. It also has limitations as a result of side effects such as sedation, drowsiness, reduction in motor coordination, and a high risk of developing impairment.

There is also a high possibility of a withdrawal symptom appearing even after a short term administration of the drug, could be less than four months duration. The severity of withdrawal depends on the dosage, half-life, potency, duration of the treatment and length of the taper period. It is also difficult for patients of panic disorder and agoraphobia to withdraw from the drug probably due to the reappearance of panic attacks as a result of the withdrawal symptoms being triggered as a result of the short period of tapering.

There is also a high rate of abuse of the drug found in patients with a history of alcohol disorder, drug or substance abuse. Patients with personality disorder or who use benzodiazepines and alcohol as a means of self-medication also have a high tendency of exhibiting abusive tendencies towards the drug.

Thus, these guidelines do not see benzodiazepines as a good fit for a first choice drug during treatments.

In the process of recommending the use of benzodiazepines, the APA guidelines of 1998 recommended that a combination of both SSRI and benzodiazepines be made in the first week of treatment. This recommendation is based on the following:

1. Some patients of panic disorder and agoraphobia are very sensitive to agoraphobia are quite sensitive to the side effects of SSRI medications leading to the appearance of anxiety, agitation, insomnia. Some of these symptoms could also increase or appear after the administration of this treatment leading patients to discontinue treatment because the drugs worsen their symptoms.

2. An SSRI compound takes four weeks to become effective.

Therefore, the administration of benzodiazepines simultaneously with the SSRI compounds in the first week of treatment could reduce the activation effect caused by the SSRI compound thus reducing the frequency and severity of panic attacks, insomnia and anticipatory attacks before the SSRI compound becomes active. The simultaneous administration of benzodiazepine is quite important in patients with a critical need for speedy control of symptoms

REFERENCES

Bandura, A., Adams, N. E., Hardy, A. B., & Howells, G. N. (1980). Tests of the generality of self-efficacy theory. Cognitive Therapy and Research, 4, 39–66.

Bandura, A., Jeffery, R. W., & Gajdos, E. (1975). Generalizing change through participant modeling with self-directed mastery. Behaviour Research and Therapy,

13, 141–152.

Bandura, A., Jeffery, R. W., & Wright, C. L. (1974). Efficacy of participant modeling as a function of response induction aids. Journal of Abnormal Psychology, 83, 56–64.

Barlow, D. H., Craske, M. G., Cerny, J. A., & Klosko, J. S. (1989). Behavioral treatment of panic disorder. Behavior Therapy, 20, 261–282.

Barlow, D. H., O'Brien, G. T., & Last, C. G. (1984). Couples treatment of agoraphobia. Behavior Therapy, 15, 41–58.

Baron, R. M., & Kenny, D. A. (1986). The moderator–mediator variable distinction in socialpsychological research: Conceptual, strategic, and statistical considerations. Journal of Personality and Social Psychology, 51, 1173–1182.

Bitran, S., Morissette, S. B., Spiegel, D. A., & Barlow, D. H. (2008). A pilot study of sensation-focused intensive treatment for panic disorder with moderate to severe agoraphobia:Preliminary outcome and benchmarking data. Behavior Modification, 32, 196–214.

Bonn, J. A., Readhead, C. P., & Timmons, B. H. (1984). Enhanced adaptive behavioural

response in agoraphobic patients pretreated with

breathing retraining. Lancet, 324,665–669.

Botella, C., Garcʹıa-Palacios, A., Villa, H., Banos, R. M., Quero, S., Alcaniz, M., & Riva, G. (2007). Virtual reality exposure in the treatment of panic disorder and agoraphobia: A con-

trolled study. Clinical Psychology and Psychotherapy, 14, 164–175. doi:10.1002/cpp.524

Bouchard, S., Paquin, B., Payeur, R., Allard, M., Rivard, V., Fournier, T., … Lapierre,J. (2004). Delivering cognitive-behavior therapy for panic disorder with agoraphobia in videoconference. Telemedicine Journal and e-Health, 10, 13–25. doi:10.1089/153056204773644535

Bouchard, S., Payeur, R., Rivard, V., Allard, M., Paquin, B., Renaud, P., & Goyer, L. (2000). Cognitive behavior therapy for panic disorder with agoraphobia in videoconference: Preliminary results. CyberPsychology and Behavior, 3, 999–1007.

Chambless, D. L. (1990). Spacing of exposure sessions in treatment of agoraphobia and simple phobia. Behavior Therapy, 21, 217–229.

Chambless, D. L., Foa, E. B., Groves, G. A., & Goldstein, A. J. (1979). Flooding with Brevital in the treatment of agoraphobia: Countereffective Behaviour Research and Therapy, 17,243–251.

Cho, Y., Smits, J. A. J., Powers, M. B., & Telch, M. J. (2007). Do changes in panic appraisal predict improvement in clinical status following cognitive-behavioral treatment of panic disorder? Cognitive Therapy and Research, 31, 695–707.

Choi, Y.-H., Vincelli, F., Riva, G., Wiederhold, B. K., Lee, J.-H., & Park, K.-H. (2005). Effects of group experiential cognitive therapy for the treatment of panic disorder with agoraphobia. CyberPsychology and Behavior, 8, 387–393.

Clark, D. M., Salkovskis, P. M., Hackmann, A., Middleton, H., Anastasiades, P., & Gelder, M. (1994). A comparison of cognitive therapy, applied relaxation and imipramine in the treatment of panic disorder. British Journal of Psychiatry, 164, 759–769.

Clark, D. M., Salkovskis, P. M., Hackmann, A., Wells, A., Ludgate, J., & Gelder, M. (1999).

Brief cognitive therapy for panic disorder: A randomized controlled trial. Journal of Consulting and Clinical Psychology, 67 , 583–589.

Cobb, J. P., Mathews, A. M., Childs-Clarke, A., & Blowers, C. M. (1984). The spouse as co-therapist in the treatment of agoraphobia. British Journal of Psychiatry, 144, 282–287.

Codd, R. T., Twohig, M. P., Crosby, J. M., & Enno, A.

(2011). Treatment of three anxiety disorder cases with acceptance and commitment therapy in private practice. Journal of Cognitive Psychotherapy, 25, 203–217.

Craske, M. G., Rowe, M., Lewin, M., & Noriega-Dimitri, R. (1997). Interoceptive exposure versus breathing retraining within cognitive-behavioural therapy for panic disorder with agoraphobia. British Journal of Clinical Psychology, 36, 85–99.

Crowe, M. J., Marks, I. M., Agras, W. S., & Leitenberg, H. (1972). Time-limited desensitisation, implosion and shaping for phobic patients: A crossover study. Behaviour Research and Therapy, 10, 319–328.

Davis, L., Barlow, D. H., & Smith, L. (2010). Comorbidity and the treatment of principal anxiety disorders in a naturalistic sample. Behavior Therapy, 41, 296–305.

Dreessen, L., Arntz, A., Luttels, C., & Sallaerts, S. (1994). Personality disorders do not influence the results of cognitive behavior therapies for anxiety disorders. Comprehensive Psychiatry, 35, 265–274.

Eaton, W. W., Kessler, R. C., Wittchen, H. U., & Magee, W. J. (1994). Panic and panic disorder in the United States. American Journal of Psychiatry, 151, 413–420.

Emmelkamp, P. M. (1974). Self-observation versus

flooding in the treatment of agoraphobia. Behaviour Research and Therapy, 12, 229–237.

Emmelkamp, P. M., & Emmelkamp-Benner, A. (1975). Effects of historically portrayed modeling and group treatment on self-observation: A comparison with agoraphobics. Behaviour Research and Therapy, 13, 135–139.

Emmelkamp, P. M., van Dyck, R., Bitter, M., Heins, R., Onstein, E. J., & Eisen, B. (1992). Spouse-aided therapy with agoraphobics. British Journal of Psychiatry, 160, 51–56.

Everaerd, W. T., Rijken, H. M., & Emmelkamp, P. M. (1973). A comparison of "flooding" and "successive approximation" in the treatment of agoraphobia. Behaviour Research and Therapy, 11, 105–117.

Faravelli, C., & Pallanti, S. (1989). Recent life events and panic disorder. American Journal of Psychiatry, 146, 622–626.

Fava, G. A., Rafanelli, C., Grandi, S., Conti, S., Ruini, C., Mangelli, L., & Belluardo, P. (2001). Long-term outcome of panic disorder with agoraphobia treated by exposure. Psychological Medicine, 31, 891–898

Agoraphobia

CHAPTER SIX

At age 35, Sheila seemed to practically have it all. A family who loved her, a good job which paid well and she had completely paid off her mortgage and student loans. The only downside to her life was the continuous stress and anxiety she felt while at work, however it was quite normal and everyone faced these same drawbacks pr so she thought.

However, things came to a standstill as she had her first panic attack on her way driving back from work. In her words, it felt like she couldn't catch her breath and all she could do to stay alive was to try to take in deep breaths.

Her heart was beating really fast and her hands were sweaty. She felt as though she was dying and the only way she could survive was if she was able to go home. A few minutes later, the feelings subsided and shakily, she drove home and fell asleep.

She chalked this up to the pressures she was facing at work and pushed the whole experience to the back of her mind going about her daily activities as usual.

She knew it wasn't a fluke however when she experienced this the week after the first experience on her way to church. She became so scared to go out and had to call in for a sick leave. Her family was extremely worried and booked her an appointment with a therapist.

After all the tests were conducted and questions answered, she was diagnosed with agoraphobia and she was given some medications, one of which was Benzodiazepine. However, she started experiencing some side effects like nausea and drowsiness and she had to stop the treatments.

On returning back to her therapist, she was then told about a method of treatment which involved meditation.

INTRODUCTION TO MEDITATION

Definition of Meditation

The word meditation was coined from the Latin word "Meditari". Meditari means to engage in reflection and contemplation. The word meditation is derived from the same greek and latin roots as the word medicine. Manocha in the year 2000 defined meditation as "a discrete and well-defined experience of a state of thoughtful awareness or mental silence in which the activity of the mind is reduced without lessening the power of psycho alertness"

It was also defined by Walsh and Shapiro in the year 2006 as "a family of self-regulation practices that aim to bring mental processes under voluntary control through focusing attention and awareness"

Other descriptions of the term meditation often emphasizes some key components examples of which are relaxation, altered awareness state, focus and concentration, process of thought and an attitude of self observation.

in 2004, a new description of the term was developed by Cardoso to encompass both clinical and traditional information. They defined meditation as any practice that

- Makes use of a specific and well defined method
- Involves relaxation of the muscles in the process
- Involves relaxation of the logic that is, anything that is done without the intention of analysing the psychophysical effects, judging the likely results or even creating any expectation regarding the process.
- It is induced by one's self
- It involves the use of a skill of focusing on one's self.

HISTORY OF MEDITATION

During the year 500 BCE, the historical Buddha, Sakyamuni stepped into a new phase-the religious life. He was apparently aware of some meditation techniques which were already practiced by some cultures in south Asia where deep thinking was a part of the culture.

Historical sources originating from that period are often unclear in their descriptions of some of the contemplative cultures of these people. However, one can decipher some new trends.

These cultures believed that the life of deep thinking should be focused on an inward search for one's true self (it was called the atman). The true self was assumed to be hidden by one's extreme involvement on a world ruled by the sense; many of these practices involved a focus inward whereby we stepped away from the use of the senses. In addition to this focus inward, most practices aimed at reducing instances of other different types of information termed as "conceptuality" (kalpama) which was believed to obstruct one's view of true self.

Some of the distractions believed to have been caused by the instability of one's mind were believed to have a link to the breath fluctuation causing meditative techniques to either have a form of breathing control or attention placed on breath predisposition. The mind was also believed to be affected by the body thus making these practices take on some specific postures and exercises.

When Sakyamuni implemented some of these practices, the context shifted as a result of the fact that the Buddha stood by the belief that the term "a true self" was wrong. Even though Buddha changed some of the practices he had encountered, the methods developed by he and his followers kept some of the fundamental principles of inward focus, breathing importance and importance of the body.

It could be that the main style of Buddhist meditation which describes these concepts is meditation which is done with an aim of improving concentration. This type of meditation is aimed at achieving a state called samatha. This is a state where the participant is able to keep their focus on one object for an unspecified period of time. It could be described as one of the earliest styles of Buddhist meditation which aims at attaining that peaceful state.

This method increases a mental capacity known as "smriti" which can be described as both "mindfulness"and "awareness". Simply, it can be defined as the ability of the brain to determine if smrti is focused on the intended subject or if the attention of the subject has moved elsewhere.

There is also another faculty of the brain called samprajanya which uses a type of mental self-awareness. The awareness isn't focused on the object this time around however; it Is placed on the intentional relation itself.

Samatha provides the basic formula for other Buddhist practices, as it provides the basic viewpoint for any other practice which places a really focused concentration on a specified object. However, this method in itself is not quite Buddhist as the development of the practices involved in samatha does not lead to all the changes required by the buddhists especially when it comes to controlling emotions. Though the samatha style of meditation is a major part of Buddhist deep-thinking traditions, it has to be accompanied by some other major style of Buddhist meditation called the vipasyana.

The vipasayana is a style of practice which was used

earlier alongside the samatha. It is a style of meditation which when used in combination with the sense of stability and focus gotten from the samatha style of practice; it enables the participant to gain insight into one's habit and assumptions especially about topics such as identity and emotion.

This understanding includes a deeper meaning into the meaning of selflessness.It involves the realisation that one's belief in a fixed, identity is not correct thus causing the emotional habits that reflect the beliefs to be baseless.

However, there is diversity in the way the way vipasyana is defined and included into practice. Some traditions believe that reasoning and an expression of internal concepts are very important to the practice while some other traditions believe that concepts alongside reason are not important in attaining vipasyana.

Some other cultures believe that vipasyana meditation has to have an object to focus on during which a form of analysis comes to the forefront. Other cultures believe that this form of meditation requires no object.

FURTHER HISTORICAL DEVELOPMENTS OF MEDITATION

Though the combination of both vipasyana and samatha provides a historical foundation for the development of Contemplative practices in the Buddhist community, there were other forms of meditation which were developed in the Buddhist communities of Asia. There are three practices in Indian culture which are a representative of these range of developments. They are:

- Recollection of Buddha Meditations (Buddhanusmrti)
- Meditation of lovingkindness (Maitribhavana)
- Tantric Meditations (Wind Meditations)

Recollection of Buddha Meditations: This could have been one of the oldest Buddha practices and it involves reciting aloud the characteristics of the Buddha and during its starting period, it might not have really been more than that.

At a point, it developed into visualising the Buddha in the space in front of the participant while reciting his attributes aloud.

This technique of visualisation and reciting is similar to a range of other Buddhist practices that came about during the first millennium. One of these major practices included the practice of visualising deities and surreal environments.

Meditation of loving kindness: This was also a common practice during the earlier and later Buddhism periods. It is termed "the cultivation of the great compassion" (mahakaruma). This purpose of this practice is to help the participant reach an emotional state of love and compassion towards all beings.

This practice is a representative of all states that either promotes or inhibits attitudes by inducing a certain emotional state. This practice could involve visualisation and recitation just like in the recitation practice. Other strategies such as thinking through the steps as a plea for compassion could also be employed.

Tatric Wind Meditation: This was the last to develop in India; it was formed during the end of the first millennium. These practices involve manipulating the various forms of energy which are called wind metaphorically. These winds are alleged to flow in channels all through the body.

This model is strangely similar to the theory of the nervous system propagated during recent times where the theory of wind Is similar to that of neural impulses.

In this Buddhist practice, the mind is thought to be comprised of the wind energy and any practice that manipulated its energy was done with an aim of induce or reduce mental strength and tricks.

Some of the techniques included the visualisation of some certain points in the body and certain syllables which aimed at altering the flow of mental energy using physical exercises (breathing exercises included) and other techniques which included diet change.

One of the examples of thi styles of meditation included the Tummo, a method which was believed that when performed not only manipulates the wind but generate body heat as a byproduct.

THEORY OF MEDITATION

With an aim of aiding the mastery of techniques used in meditation, and also respond critics outside their culture, Buddhist theorists in india developed detailed accounts of their meditative practices. Some of these accounts are usually complex and not easily explained using neuroscience.

The theory of meditation is addressed in the form of practices which strengthens samatha and vipasyanya practices using these two practices to describe two different facets of the same state of meditation. The theory is derived from the Tibetian Buddhism.

Using the theory pushed forward by their Indian ancestors, Tibetian Buddhists reached a conclusion that the highest forms of Buddhist Meditation must combine the properties of Samatha and Vipasyanya into one single practice.

A metaphor used to describe this was an illustration that a practitioner cannot make any advancement spiritually without the integration of both Samatha and Vipasanya similar to the way a cart cannot move without its two wheels. Another metaphor used was the illustration that when attempting to see the murals in a dark cave, one must use a lamp which is simultaneously well-covered and bright. If the lamp is not well-covered, there is a possibility that the lamp will flicker out or even die out and if the lamp's light is not intense enough, you would become unable to see the mural.

This explains both styles of meditation in that samatha mainly concerns the stability of the meditative state while vipasyanya refers to the intensity of the state.

To explain this, stability means the degree in which a participant is able to place complete attention on the object without interruption. In reference to such states, clarity refers to the sharpness of the appearance of the object in question.

The two states are often believed to be at odds, especially in cases of novice mediators. In the case of a novice, the greater the stability of the meditative state, the lesser the intensity will be.

These two states are often expressed using terms like dullness and excitement. When dullness first begins, the concentration and focus on the object will be maintained, however, after some time, a feeling of drowsiness takes over and the clarity is affected or in an extreme case, the person might even fall asleep. In a reverse situation, when there is a high level of excitement, the clarity of the object will often increase but the intensity and excitement will disturb the meditative process causing a rise in distractions.

In an ideal meditative state, there is a balance between both states of excitement and dullness thus making it hard to describe the term 'meditation' as relaxation in both the tibetian culture and other Buddhist cultures.

This is not to deny the technique that makes the participant relax, these techniques aid to reduce the level of excitement which ultimately improves the meditation process. However, an excess usage of such techniques is likely to lull the practitioner into a state of drowsiness. This is why not many Buddhist practices are done in a lying position.

Another thing to take note of is the techniques used to counter the effect of both relaxation and dullness.

While it is known that the balance of both clarity and intensity forms the template for the Tibetian Buddhist practice, it is quite essential to understand the ways these templates are altered for the other different practices.

An example of this are the beginners who aim to learn the meditative state of Open Presence (Rigpa Chogzag) could be taught the art of placing emphasis on one feature or another to make headway in the study of the practice. One of the main advice they are encouraged to follow is that it is easier to make mistakes in the stage of clarity because it is more important to avoid dullness especially in the beginning phases of their training.

Another issue raised by the practice of the Open Presence is the ease of application of the model to meditations that doesn't require an object to focus on. In meditations where objects are not required, stability is often referred to as the ease with which the meditator is disturbed out of the state the meditation is supposed to bring on.

To crown it all, one final theory of the theory of meditation is regarding the differences between the actual meditative state and the state after meditation. The state of meditation the participant/meditator was in is said to lead to a post meditative state. One perspective of post-meditative way is that it continues even in the post meditatie state. In other words, the post-meditative state include behaviour change.

TYPES OF MEDITATION

There are many meditation techniques being

practiced currently. Some of such meditation types such as the tatric meditation, loving kindness meditation. These types of meditation however are grouped into two different categories. They are:

- Mindfulness Meditation

- Concentration meditation

This type of meditation has been explained briefly in the beginning of this chapter. However, we are going to be explaining these meditation types in detail.

Mindfulness meditation:

This Is also called the insight meditation. It has a huge part in understanding the benefit of meditation as related to therapeutic growth along with personal development. the difference between mindfulness technique and other meditation techniques is the development of an ability which allows the participant to maintain a non-judgemental and sustained awareness on the desired objects of attention.

This type of meditation allows attention to span broader resulting in a higher and broader without further analysis and deep thinking. This type of meditation uses any source of attention be It emotions, physical sensations or even an image.

Mindfulness meditation has an association with contributions of people from America who joined the monastery in countries like Asia, thai theravartc.

One influential teacher from Asia is Thich Naht Han a monk from Vietnam. He is interested in the art of combining long kindness meditation and contemplative walking as one component of meditation

Another thing to note is that while the Zen tradition is not often described as an integral part of mindfulness meditation, some aspects of the Zen techniques play central roles in modern day meditation practices.

Mindfulness meditation cultivates the moment-moment awareness of one's present situation. The scope of visualisation could either be broad or narrow. This is done with the aim of growing a stable awareness of one's internal and external environment. This is often said to positively benefit some areas such as emotional balance, regulation of behaviour, physical awareness, relaxation and relationship with other people. Improvement in some of these areas decreases the feeling of stress felt

BASIC ELEMENTS OF MINDFULNESS MEDITATION

Mindfulness meditation techniques is segregated into three main aspects: breath awareness, open focus mindfulness and guided mindfulness.

Breath Awareness

The southeast Asian school of mindfulness meditation which was made popular by Kornfield, Salberg had a technique of focusing on their breathing as a means to both realign and engage the attention when they get caught up on attention.

The principle here is that the breath is a major determining force of stress which not only serves serving not only to reduce activity but also a positive physiological response.

Open Awareness

This is usually called the main part of mindfulness meditation. It is done with an aim to increase awareness both bodily and mentally, disengage the emotional and analytical parts of the brain, and retrain the tendencies to engage in mindfulness easily during daily activities.

Guided Awareness

In this practice of mindfulness meditation, the content is important and engages one part of self but in a mindful way. In traditional practices, the focus might be on chants or feelings of compassion. However, in physical situations, the focus is usually on physical sensations such as hunger, or stress. The goal is to change the behavioural and emotional reaction to some of these experiences.

They can be incorporated into healing and therapeutic approaches in different ways: as part of the general mindfulness programs or they could be used as scripted programs. Scripted meditations doesn't need to be something long, a brief loving kindness meditation can be effective. It could also be the instructions used in the psoriasis treatment tape.

One of the most useful practices is considering practices which are focused on the body as a form of guided awareness exercise. An example of such is yoga, which originates from the word 'yuj' –meaning to yoke (both mind and body together). Other examples include body scanning, walking meditation and guided meditation using interoceptive experience.

Practice length:

To get the most out of the mindfulness meditation practice, there is a need to set aside a certain amount of time, maybe thirty to forty minutes, once or twice every day. Shorter practice periods of about 10 to 20 minutes in a day can be beneficial when teaching children how to meditate but it is not enough time to get the mind to move to its absorptive state. There is a gradual integration of the mindfulness experience through an awareness of each happening moment. These mini-meditations may become a powerful sort of practice.

2, CONCENTRATION MEDITATION

This meditation technique is founded on balance and moderation. This involves a level of self-discipline. In Hundu, self-discipline is referred to a stapas and they believe that unless the heat of self-discipline is present in our lives burying all the limitations of our system, it will be difficult to encounter illumination.

The mind falls into three states: the dull state, overactive state and the calm, centered state. This is similar to the three matter qualities Guna (called the Tamas, Rajas and Sattwa in the Sanskrit. The first quality is that of darkness, lethargy, inertia etc, The second quality is synonymous to excessive ambition, egotism, discontent and arrogance

According to Swami Paramanda, there is no concentration without meditation. He believes that when a man has achieved his full state of readiness through singleness, he becomes meditative. The major aim of the concentrated meditation is the attainment of the concentrated state of Ekagra.

Concentration meditation involves focusing the main attention on an object. If that is attained, the ability to steady and focus your mind on a thought steadily for twelve seconds, it is Dhyana or meditation and each of them will result in Sandhi. Another type of concentration meditation is inward focus. This involves focusing on

The aim of this practice is to align with the object desired and disunite the mind from disturbing influences. It is also important to know that if a person practices just concentration meditation without a little bit of mindfulness attached to it, the person might begin suffering from delusions and other side effects. There are three stages of concentration meditation and they include the following:

1. Concentration:

The metaphor used to explain this class is 'Before an instrument used, it must be created'. This is an unchanging, stable focus on the chosen or idea given emphasis to excluding other objects. Oftentimes, there is a need for really stressful exercises to develop the ability to focus unwaveringly on one object in both thoughts and physically.

This stage however has no ethical and spiritual setting. in other words, there is no special timeframe or location and thus can be done at any place, posture or time for practicing.

2. Lower meditation:

This stage of meditation is synonymous to the dedication of newly created instrument to useful work. Some of the examples include bodily meditation based on the fundamental doctrines taught by Buddha-Karma, oneness of life, rebirth, three fires, and three signs of being. It is said that a perfect mind has monopoly over these subjects. This class also deals with character building, four building viharas and an intentional rising of consciousness.

3. Higher Meditation:

There is a subtle shift within that commonly takes place after experiencing stage one and stage two of the meditation process. They would be in the world however, not of the world. They find out that objects undergo a transcending process and names and definitions are left behind.

This sub division consist of the janas talked about in the Buddhist scripture. This division blinds higher mysticism and a deep understanding of pure abstract.

4. CONTEMPLATION:

This is the highest stage of meditation and healing process. It is an involvement with reality and an absorption into nature.

There are a few exercises which can be performed to aid in the cultivation of a mind which is able to concentrate and focus

1. Get physically fit: The physical brain is the route for consciousness to function and unless the body is at

its peak condition, the brain isn't going to function at its normal capabilities. There is a yoga saying which states 'The key to yoga lies in the lower bowel' and the use of pure water to purify the system goes a long way. After getting fit, you have to learn to maintain it by giving up one or more of the toxic foods which your body doesn't necessarily require and also refuse to weaken the body by giving in to its desires to become lax and indulge in physical pleasures.

2. Concentrate on the current task at hand: There is a need to develop a single minded concentration on whatever task you have at hand. A saying by a student of meditation went like this "Before a person can meditate, he/she has to have learnt the art of concentration otherwise while there might be an overabundance of will and inspiration, there will be a lack of something equally as important-the technique". One of the key ways to achieve this is to state what needs to be done (everything which needs to be done has to have a purpose) and then eliminate all other unnecessary and mindless activities which can hamper the achievement of such purposeful goals.

3. Clarify every issue and master each act:

Research shows that most people do not use a huge part of their mental capacity especially when it comes to processes like thinking. In depth thinking Is something that has to be learnt just as maths and English are often learnt in schools. The thought process is divided into two-facts and ideas and not many people are able to necessarily think out an idea and convey it in the best way possible. Humans have been conditioned for so long to have some pre-conditioned responses for some certain kind of stimulus and this is often what we fall back on without predetermining and thinking.

To change this however, there has to be more thinking before engaging in any action and determine why that action has to be performed. This is done with the aim of making every activity done more effective and efficient.

4. Control reactions to emotions and mass opinions:

There has to be a distinction between your thoughts and the external thoughts. Before any thought moves you towards action, you have to determine if the thought is a deeply thought out opinion of yours or if it's just a reflection of the views of the news people, or the people around you. Most times it's often hard to keep personal opinions especially if they go against the popular opinion of the media and the people around us. There has to be a mental filter placed around the thoughts coming into our mind. There also has to be a tight leash on your emotional response. There is a need to decide your personal reaction and control reactions such as anger or pain.

EFFECTS OF MEDITATION

PSYCHOLOGICAL EFFECTS:

There are many cognitive benefits associated with meditation practices. Some of these abilities could either be normal or paranormal. A lot of research has been done to discover the benefits of meditation on behaviour.

-Perceptual Ability

In the year 1984, there was a research conducted by Brown, Forte and Dysant on sensitivity to visual stimuli using Buddhist meditation practitioners as a sample. The design control of the experiment was a before and after model. The post test was conducted three months after serious exercise and the eve of sensitivity was measured using simple flashes of light. There was an improvement in the sensitivity of vision after the meditation exercise. Some other studies show an improvement in visual imagery alongside improved attention ability.

Memory and intelligence

In the year 1986, Jedrczak proved that the time spent practicing transcendental meditation is directly proportional to the high performance on nonverbal test. Students of meditation often have higher grades, increased learning ability, improved short and long term memory as compared to their peers.

Creativity

Recently, researchers reported an improved level of creativity with meditation exercises. Another main importance of meditation is self actualisation. In 1991, some researchers named Alexandar, Gederoos and Rainfort conducted a meta-analysis on transcendental meditation using factors such as meditation, perspective of the self and the word and also a strong sense of self. They found out that it had a great benefit on self actualisation

Emotion:

Studies have shown that there was a great improvement in mood, anxiety and well-being in a lot of individuals who were involved in mindfulness meditation exercises. One of the main reasons for engaging in meditation exercises especially mindfulness meditation practice is relieving emotional distress caused by the problems of treatment or numbing fear caused by a disability or threats of death.

It is powerful for patients who suffer from cancer. It

is also highly beneficial for people such as medical students or business executives who work in really stressful environments. One of the main processes of Tibetian Buddhism is adopting a positive emotional response.

It was documented that meditation exercises increases activity to a limited degree in the left prefrontal cortex of the brain that is in charge of positive emotion. Mindfulness meditation is also beneficial in treating patients who suffers from borderline personality disorder. It also seems to be a good cure for anger as awareness, acceptance and suspense of any action going on at the moment of anger is one of the key principles taught in mindfulness meditation.

Behaviour:

Meditation practice can be beneficial in areas of behaviour as a result of some of the following factors: enhancing emotional regulation, sowing behaviour sequence as a result of awareness cultivation, increased acceptance of behaviour and lifestyle recommendations or tolerating and riding out craving feelings rather than impulsive response.

Most of the behavioural changes which come about as a result of the meditation and mindfulness technique is due to a deconditioning process (freedom from patterns of compulsion and avoidance) resulting in purposeful and wise actions. However, for a behaviour goal to occur there has to be an implicit focus on the behaviour goals.

One of the ways in which this technique is particularly beneficial to the mindfulness participant is through improvement in their eating behaviour and food choices. Another effect is the reduction in the usage of alcohol and drugs as a result of practicing mindfulness meditation. These benefits are accompanied with impulse control improvement, optimism and a handle on their level of control.

MEDITATION AND IMPROVED SELF ACCEPTANCE

A high amount of stress is linked to harsh self-judgement and a result of this is the inability to make a social connection. One of the main goals of meditation originally was to improve levels of self-acceptance. According to Walsh and Shapiro, one of the fundamental processes of meditation is identification which refers to observing experiences without making them all about you. It is a type of disengagement.

There is also a research done proving that experienced mediators in the mindfulness tradition portrayed a greater sense of self-acceptance when faced with stress compared to other non-participants. Another group of individuals who went through the Zazen training in 1996, a study conducted by Lesh.

PHYSIOLOGICAL EFFECTS OF MEDITATION

Meditation has been found to have some noteworthy effects on human physiology. Some of the physiologic benefits are:

- Meditation and heart rate:

Some studies show that the heart slows down during meditation and increases rapidly during meditation. Meditation practices such as transcendental meditation, zen, relaxation response and some other relaxation techniques have been found to decrease the heart rate. However only long term practitioners show obvious difference in heart rate.

- Meditation and high blood pressure:

One of the variables which can easily be measured

is blood pressure. Research conducted proves that meditation lowers blood pressure for people who are mildly or moderately hypertensive. However, further studies show that this disappears once practice stops.

Meditation and Respiration:

Research shows that oxygen consumption is decreased sometimes up to 50% during meditation. There is also a quicker elimination rate of carbon dioxide alongside a reduction of the rate of respiration.

Meditation and Skin resistance

Low skin resistance which is determined by galvanic skin response is a main stress indicator. Among participants of transcendental meditation, there has been a discovery showing high skin resistance.

EFFECT OF MEDITATION ON AGORAPHOBIA

There are three main self-help practices which are currently used in the treatment of anxiety and anxiety disorders.

One of the researches conducted was published in 1992 by Jon and his colleagues. This experiment involved picking out patients who qualified and ticked out the DSM-III and DSM-IV classification of anxiety disorders of which agoraphobia was a part of. After this, selected patients were referred and screened in order to participate in the study. Those who passed the screening were then invited to meet with a psychiatrist or psychologist who diagnosed them within the subset of panic disorder with or without agoraphobia.

Participants in the study were encouraged to attend a 2 hour weekly classes for a period of 8 weeks alongside a meditation retreat which was about 7 hours long in the sixth week of the experiment. Patients were expected to practice both formal and informal meditation exercises which were discussed weekly in class. The results of the experiment showed a decline in the Hamilton panic scores assessment between the period of pretreatment and post treatment.

Another research conducted by Camila and Bernard in 2014 highlighted the effect of yoga which is a mindfulness meditation technique and cognitive therapy on patients with panic disorder. In this method, twenty patients who fell into the category of panic disorder with or without agoraphobia according to the DSM IV classification were grouped into two- group one were treated with yoga alone and group two were treated with both yoga and cognitive behavioural therapy for a period of two months.

The results showed an improvement in panic and panic related symptoms such as anxiety, bodily sensations and other symptoms in both groups which proved the effectiveness of yoga in the treatment of panic disorder symptoms.

WHAT HAPPENS IN THE BRAIN DURING MEDITATION THAT CAUSES LESSENING OF PANIC

A regular activation of the sympathetic nervous system alongside the hypothalamic pituitary axis has often been linked as the main cause of stress, anxiety and depression. One of the main reasons for the reduction of stress, anxiety and the overall relaxation experienced after meditation (yoga) practice is the reduced SNS activity, arousal and activation of antagonistic limbic and neuromuscular system. Meditation practice is often found to reduce cortisol level, catecholamine secretion, basal metabolic rate and oxygen consumption.

Meditation also has a regulatory effect on breathing leading to an overall relaxation feeling experienced alongside stress and breathing relief. This is because one of the main teachings in meditation (mindfulness) practice is breathing control which helps to control the activity between the sympathetic and parasympathetic nervous system.

Meditation also increases the level of vagal influence in the body. The polyvagal theory states that physiological states enhance different kinds of behaviour. Example, a physiological state which leads to a vagal withdrawal could cause the flight or fight reaction while the enhancement of vagal influence leads to an improvement in the level of social engagement exhibited. This is because the vagal pathway of the body made up of the parasympathetic nerve fibers increase their influence on the body causing a normalization of heart rate.

Another benefit of the breathing techniques taught in mindfulness meditation is the desensitization of CO_2 chemoreceptors in the brain thus leading them to respond to the CO_2 increase when exhaling until the individual reaches a point where they are able to exhale and still reduce the heartbeat.

Thus, the research studied showed that there is a reduced chance of meditation practitioners to develop anxiety disorders and react better when the negative symptoms when they appear.

ABOUT THE AUTHOR

Demetra Harlington

- **<u>MEDITATION FOR A LEADER:</u>** Meditation to Increase Happiness - Finding Mindfulness at Work - How to Live Stress-Free and in the Moment
- **<u>How to handle anxiety and fear:</u>** Everyday Routine To Keep Anxiety At Bay - Overcoming Fear and Worry - Find Your Way Out of Depression, Anxiety, Anger and Fear
- **<u>Meditation to develop Talent:</u>** Unlock your talent with Meditation

Agoraphobia

.